Financial Excellence

A Treasury of Wisdom
and Inspiration

Financial Excellence

A Treasury of Wisdom
and Inspiration

by
John Avanzini

Harrison House
Tulsa, Oklahoma

Financial Excellence—
A Treasury of Wisdom and Inspiration

ISBN 0-89274-918-0

Harrison House
P.O. Box 35035
Tulsa, Oklahoma 74153

Contents

Introduction

This book represents the wisdom and God-given inspiration I have gained concerning Christian finances over the last several years.

What I have learned about God's plan for His children's financial well-being has come from more than thirty years of Bible study. In some cases, God has shown me some very basic truths through special revelation of His Word.

I have seen God's desire and financial plan for us plundered — individually and for the Church as a whole. The devil has continually robbed Christians who do not understand their God-given authority over him. However, I have also seen knowledge and right action triumph over the deceiver, in my life and the lives of many others.

Our Heavenly Father's plan for our finances is three-fold:

1) to provide for His children's needs,

2) to provide for the preaching of the gospel, and

3) to provide plenty for His children so that they can give joyfully to others.

This book is written to accomplish two purposes:

1) to help those who need an immediate turn-around in their personal finances to be blessed of God, so that they can be a blessing to others, and

2) to assist those who are already enjoying the Lord's financial blessings to be an even greater blessing to others.

This book is divided into three parts, combining needed general information with practical, step-by-step instruction.

Part I gives an overview of God's desire and plan for your financial abundance, as well as information about just how the devil will try to rob you, often before that abundance even reaches your hands! You need to know your enemy to fight him effectively!

Part II outlines God's plan, requirements, and laws for reaping the financial harvest you need or want. You will see how tithes and offerings are essential to obeying the laws of the harvest.

Part III speaks of debt — about how and why we enter into it, the special responsibility it holds for Christians, and specific suggestions as to how we can reduce and eliminate it while we wait to reap the full harvests God has promised us.

It is my sincere prayer that this book will be a blessing to you, and that you will use the knowledge in it to help others prosper and be blessed.

John Avanzini

Part I
God, Your Finances,
and the Thief

1
God Wants Abundance for Us

Child of God, I alert you to the fact that Satan is clearly waging a battle of containment against the saints of God. He is not concerned nearly so much with driving you backwards as he is with *containing* you where you are, and keeping you from getting where God wants you to go. Can you identify with that?

In your prayer life, if you desire a greater walk with God, you will find that the devil will let you continue to pray at your current prayer level. As soon as you try to break into a new dimension of prayer, frequent distractions occur. People come to visit you. Your hours change at work. The phone rings. Any time you start to move decisively forward, Satan increases his *battle of containment.*

You may have experienced this containment in the realm of holiness or sanctification. You achieve a certain walk, then you stop growing. You do not especially go backwards, but you just find it increasingly difficult to move forward. Please understand, *that is the stark reality of Satan's battle of containment* against you!

As you start to grow in the revelations I am bringing to you in this book, you will quickly realize that at this very moment, the devil is waging a powerful battle of containment in your finances. He will tell you that *you are getting along okay, so just don't rock the boat!* He will even try to deceive you into thinking that this book is just another prosperity message, *but do not be distracted!*

Please recognize that this is the *vital biblical message* your spirit-man has been hungering after, the message of deliverance from insufficiency! Do not let the devil continue to contain you in your present financial dilemma!

The Truth You Know

One of the primary deceptions so many Christians believe is that the Bible says, the truth will set you free. *The Bible does not say the truth will set you free.* The Bible says something very different. Read carefully what it actually says:

> **And ye shall *know* the truth, and the truth shall make you free.**
> **John 8:32**

Do you see it? It is *the truth you know* that has the divine power to set you free. Please hear me. The only truth that can set you free is the truth *that you personally know.* You can walk around with the truth (the Bible) in your right hand, placed lovingly over your breast; you can walk around with that precious Bible right over your lungs, and still have a horrible cancer grow in those lungs that will eventually snuff out your very life.

Many Christians die prematurely in the presence of truth, with the Bible on the nightstand next to their death bed. Keep this thought in mind. The *presence* of truth cannot and does not heal! You see, it is not the presence of truth, but *the knowledge of truth* that has power and sets you free. Hear the Scripture:

> **And ye shall *know* the truth, and the truth shall make you free.**
> **John 8:32**

It is time to order our lives line upon line, precept upon precept, concept upon biblical concept. We must build a foundation of truth so powerful that Satan cannot contain it.

Now hear me well. I want you to break out of the containment building that Satan has constructed around your finances. However, please be careful not to mistake *a mere penetration* of Satan's containment in your finances *as a breakthrough.* There is a vast difference between a penetration and a breakthrough, and I want nothing less for you from this book than a *total breakthrough!*

Perhaps you have made an occasional penetration in the wall of containment Satan has placed around your finances. Maybe you have already gained enough bits and pieces of knowledge to understand that God does not intend for you to be poor, and that He has a biblical plan of abundance for your life.

I want you to go beyond bits and pieces. It is time for you to start gathering *great quantities* of spiritual power. When this power is complete, it will bring about a *total breakthrough* in your finances which will move you permanently beyond Satan's containment!

Remember, any time you want to break through a spiritual barrier, *it takes great spiritual energy;* it takes the power of God working through you! The breakthrough comes only when you allow that energy, that input of biblical truth, to continue and continue to grow. It literally takes a violent effort, not casual daydreaming and wishing, to accomplish it.

The same energy that has brought you previous breakthroughs, the same level of effort that has swept you to past victories, must now come forth for you to achieve a financial breakthrough as you are guided by this book. You must *gather* many biblical principles and *apply* them, not so that you can make just a little hole and peer through a small, rapidly closing penetration, but so that you can achieve nothing less than a *total breakthrough!*

Satan has contained you in your finances long enough! Jericho's walls must come down! As you understand the *truth* of this powerful revelation, as you *know* this truth by putting it into *practical application* in your life, you will experience a powerful new day in your finances.

If there is still any doubt that Satan is containing you in your finances, let me quickly prove to you that he is. Right now, you can think of several people who are not as smart nor qualified as you are who are making more money than you make. How can this be unless the devil has put an invisible wall around your financial potential? You see, the devil does not care how much money non-Christians make, because as long as they control it, their money will not be used to finance the preaching of the gospel.

The rock stars will never finance the gospel. The raunchy movie producers will not give one dime for the next major evangelistic crusade. That's why the devil does not contain them as he does you and me!

You see, financing the end-time harvest is up to you and me as born-again Christians. If you do not have the financial breakthrough God wants you to have, His Church will never rise to the full level of the vision He has for it.

The only way to smash and destroy the wall of containment around your finances is through a violent, highly energetic act on your part.

I don't use the word *violent* at my choosing, but God's Word literally tells us to get violent and use our God-given force (spiritual energy).

**And from the days of John the Baptist until now the kingdom of heaven suffereth violence, and *the violent take it by force.*
Matthew 11:12**

If you want to make a breakthrough in your finances, then determine right now that you are going to take *whatever action is necessary* to crush the devil's wall of containment around you, breaking through by force and violence into a new level of understanding *and* knowledge in the area of your finances.

All of a sudden, you will realize that God's Word is concentrated so strongly in you that you have enough spiritual energy to come with *violent spiritual force* against the invisible wall that is resisting you and pushing against your finances, and blow that wall asunder!

You will charge forth into newly discovered wealth and prosperity, *receiving literally more than enough* to help finance every worthwhile Christian ministry that God directs you to help.

I think you can now see that if you really want this financial breakthrough, it will take more than a penetration. Although you have hungered for this breakthrough, you probably never have possessed enough of the spiritual power, the concentrated energy, to break out of those satanic walls of containment, into true biblical, financial success and freedom.

Child of God, you are at a critical point. Now is the time for *your* breakthrough! Read. Study. Absorb. Then take *violent action!* Begin to seize the financial power you have according to the Word of God!

Get Violent in God

"Why is violent action necessary?" you might ask.

You see, those old teachings and traditions about being poor have made the Word of God about abundance ineffective for you. This verse is a good example:

> **But thou shalt remember the Lord thy God:**
> **for it is he that giveth thee *power to get wealth*. . . .**
> **Deuteronomy 8:18**

When was the last time you heard anyone give a sermon on *that* scripture? You see, there are walls around that scripture containing the Church's financial advancement and expansion.

Many of you were brought up in a day when poverty was erroneously deemed by well-meaning preachers and

14

teachers to be glorious and godly. Unfortunately, the "poverty is holy" doctrine still hangs around in the back of your mind today. Many of you *still believe* there is something wrong with a man who has a lot of money.

I used to think, "Oh, God, if I just had enough. Lord, just give me enough to provide for my wife, Pat, and our kids."

Have you ever prayed a prayer like that? Sure you have, but don't ever pray it again! As this book progresses, I will show you that it is impossible for you to be *the Christian God intends for you to be* with "just enough."

Think about the day you got saved. Your salvation was absolutely free. It did not cost you one penny to get saved. I remember walking into the First Baptist Church of Largo, Florida. They treated me like a king. There was not a charge for anything. My salvation did not cost me one cent.

However, when I came back saved the next Wednesday night, and from that day on, I have been handing out money for the gospel everywhere I go!

Child of God, do you understand what I am talking about here? It costs money to bring in God's harvest, and the Church of our Lord and Savior will never have enough to do it if the saints have *just enough.* We can bring in the end-time harvest only if God's saints learn how to have *more than enough* to supply the funds needed to do the great work God has put before us.

Let's begin generating some spiritual energy in the area of your finances. Let's begin right now by destroying

15

one old concept that must go from your mind before you can move any further in your finances.

Let's establish this new thought in your mind: *There is nothing wrong with my family and me living the good life! It is God's portion for me.*

> Behold that which I have seen: it is good and comely for one to eat and to drink, and *to enjoy the good of all of his labor* that he taketh under the sun all the days of his life, which God giveth him: *for it is his portion.*
> Every man also to whom God hath given *riches and wealth,* and hath given him power to eat thereof, and *to take his portion,* and to rejoice in his labor; *this is the gift of God.*
> **Ecclesiastes 5:18,19**

The good life is your portion!

Most Christians get it in their minds that there is great insufficiency in the world, and that we must live all of our lives in that insufficiency. Let me assure you, that is not God's way. He says, "There is more than enough." He says, "The good life is your portion!"

Do you see how Satan is waging a battle of containment in your mind? It is hard for many to grasp just having enough, let alone grasping that God intends for you to have *more than enough.*

Remember, it is the world's method to have its population operate in insufficiency, shortage, and want. They feel that's the way to keep prices up—through contrived, manipulated shortage!

Do not forget, we are not of this world, and our God and King declares that the basis of His Kingdom is *abundance!* He plainly says:

> ... I am come that they might have life, and
> that they might have it *more abundantly.*
> **John 10:10**

You see, the lifestyle God has chosen for us *is* His abundance. This abundant lifestyle is the type of breakthrough you are heading for if you do not let the devil contain you through distractions, and keep you away from *knowing* the truth of God's Word that I am teaching you.

Oh, saint of God, press on, and you will stomp on the devil. God says the devil will soon be bruised under your feet:

> **And the God of peace shall bruise Satan
> under your feet shortly.**
> **Romans 16:20**

Notice the last portion of Ecclesiastes 5:19 says that the good life is your portion, it is "the gift of God," and you have the power to eat your portion.

I can just hear some of you saying, "Well, Brother John, if wealth and the good life are God's gifts to me, then why don't I have them?"

If you know anything about God, you know that He does not hand out all of His gifts on a silver platter. A good illustration of God's nature is seen when He "gave" the Promised Land to Israel. It was a gift, but they had to *fight violently* to receive it. There was not one square foot that came easily, yet Scripture clearly states it was God's gift to them.

God has set aside a portion of the world's wealth for you. It is yours for the taking. To take control of that wealth involves your decision to *fight violently* and take it out of the control of God's enemies, just as Israel took the Promised Land from the enemies of God. (Please notice that this fight is in the spirit world. I am not advocating an armed conflict.)

Notice through this personal illustration how important it is to know the truth if you expect to be set free by that truth. In my early ministry, I was Dr. John Avanzini, pastor of a fundamental, denominational church. I had a narrow view of Scripture and believed my denomination was right about every single doctrine. I was so narrow-minded, I could look through a keyhole with both eyes!

In those early ministry years, when I walked into a hospital, it was as if the hospital was having a visit from the angel of death. When I prayed for people, sometimes they would get sicker, and even die.

I did not *know* that the stripes Jesus received on my behalf and on the behalf of the world had given me *power* to lay hands on the sick so that they would have to recover. You see, you cannot walk in a truth you do not *know*.

Oh, I bought my study books in a bookstore where people knew that truth. I personally was around the truth every day. I earned a doctorate at a theological seminary, but I didn't *know* about the fullness of the Holy Ghost. You cannot have the full benefit of a truth unless you *know* it.

Finally, one day I had a breakthrough. I discovered that the Bible says, *and means,* that I could, right now in the twentieth century, lay hands on the sick and they would recover!

> . . . They shall lay hands on the sick, and
> they shall recover.
>
> **Mark 16:18**

After that discovery, pain just left people when I prayed for them. Symptoms vanished. Terminal cases were healed with a touch, one such case with just a word from the pulpit to a man diagnosed as terminal.

I experienced the difference between head knowledge and heart knowledge, the difference between *logos* and *rhema*. *Logos* is the written Word, but *rhema* is the Word of God *living* in you!

Suddenly, a whole new flow began for me! Wisdom came to me. Healing functioned through me. Once I really *knew* the truth, then I could operate in it.

Right now, you may be powerless in the area of your finances. You may be the victim of your environment which taught you that poverty is godly, and brought about a poverty atmosphere around you.

Begin now to chisel at those old, false concepts. Start this minute to begin receiving more of your financial breakthrough by absorbing the *rhema* of this incredible scripture:

> But thou shalt remember the Lord thy God:
> for it is he that giveth thee [that means you]
> power to get wealth. . . .
>
> **Deuteronomy 8:18**

Read that scripture out loud several times right now. You have very possibly never studied anything like it before. It goes against so much of what you have been taught. Yet there it is in your Bible, staring at you. Your breakthrough cannot come unless you cooperate by *violently* pressing against the restraints of Satan that make you question the validity of this Word from God. Read it again and again.

God Himself has given *you* the *power to get wealth!* Isn't that wonderful? You have the power to get wealth, and that power has been given to you by God. Say it out loud: "I have been given the power to get wealth by the God of heaven."

Say it ten times. Say it with confidence. Listen to yourself saying it. If God says this about you, then you can say it about yourself. For the rest of your life, say this to yourself several times each day, *"God has given me the power to get wealth."*

First, receive the *logos* of this statement, the written word; it *is* written in your Holy Bible (Deuteronomy 8:18).

Next, receive the *rhema* of this statement by beginning to *operate* that word in your life. To *operate the rhema* of this statement, you must understand the total context of the verse. *This understanding is very important. Do not miss a word.*

This revelation is more than the "Cadillac-faith prosperity" that has been taught in so many messages on finances. Although that message is based in a partial truth, it does not go far enough. God does not mind the saints driving Cadillacs, Lincolns, or Hondas. Yet if that's all the message you hear, then you've totally missed God! You have thrown away *the pearl* and kept the oyster shell.

Let me tell you a story about such a situation. There was a man who had been listening to the tapes of a certain prosperity preacher, and he was all excited, thinking God would make him rich, quickly.

One day he drove up to the church in a big, beautiful, new, luxury car, and parked it right in the front of the building in the most conspicuous parking space. The preacher, seeing him pull up, asked him, "Where did you get such a nice car?" to which the man replied, "Preacher, God gave me that car."

The preacher congratulated the man, and agreed with him, saying, "That looks like the kind of car God would give."

As they both walked all around the car, the preacher noticed the man's special, personalized license plate. It read, "PRAYED 4."

For the next ten to twelve months, everything seemed just great. Every Sunday, this seemingly prosperous fellow would drive up to the church in his big, beautiful, luxury car that was now affectionately being called "Old PRAYED 4." His seeming success caused some folks to feel envious, and even somewhat convicted that their faith for wealth was not at this man's level.

One Sunday, here came this same man, not in his luxury car, but this time in, of all things, an old Nash automobile. You remember how they looked. They resembled an upside-down bathtub with the windshield in the blunt end. Well, he slowly drove up in this old car and parked way in the back of the church parking lot in the most obscure parking space.

The preacher, seeing this obvious deviation from what had become his normal entrance, went over to this fellow, and asked, "Hey, where's 'Old PRAYED 4'?"

He said, "Pastor, they repossessed it, and everything else I own is in bankruptcy."

Can you imagine? They repossessed the car God had supposedly given him! Here we see the common end to the get-rich-for-your-own-benefit gospel: disappointment and loss of credibility of our witness for Christ.

The preacher of our story then put his arms around this fellow and lovingly told him, "Brother, listen to me carefully. I thank God for the teachers we have in our land, but you are obviously missing it. Come on into God's house today and start hearing what He really says about your finances, and how they relate to *His purposes,* and not how they relate to *your purposes.* Start learning the prosperity message in the proper context.

"If your motive for giving is right with God, and if you really *know* God's intentions for the prosperity you receive from Him, then if you still desire a nice car, God will give it to you. He does not mind your having a nice car if that is what you really want. However, when He gives it to you, it will be better than your last car, and you won't have to have some goofy license plate like 'PRAYED 4' on it. With the car God gives, you can have a *real* license plate, one that says 'PAID 4.' "

Establish God's Covenant

Friend, please begin to hear me on this. Deuteronomy 8:18 tells you that God has given you the *power to get wealth.* Read the verse *in context* and you will see *why* God is giving you that power!

. . . that he may establish his covenant which
he sware unto thy fathers, as it is this day.
Deuteronomy 8:18

God has given you power to get wealth so that His covenant can be established. The word *established* here means "founded and grounded financially so that no economic problems could ever uproot or overthrow the orderly operation of that covenant on the earth."

Do you really think God wants the state of the national or local economy to affect the operation of His Church and His chosen ministries? Do you really think God would want every economic slump in the natural realm to disrupt the ministry of His Church? *Of course not!*

Do you understand? God has a plan for His Church (the saints) to be so well established in finances that literally no problem in the economy will affect the church's economy: good times, bad times, depression, recession, make no difference. God intends for His Church to grow and flourish no matter what the world might be facing in its godless economics.

God has given every one of His children the *power* to get wealth so that they can be established financially to generously fund every need that arises for the operation of the covenant He made with Abraham. That alone is the primary reason the saints have been given the power to get wealth!

If you are seeking *first* the Kingdom of God and His righteousness, if you are using your God-given power to get wealth to establish God's Kingdom first, *then* the secondary portion of the covenant comes into play, which is adding all of these other things (your needs and wants) unto you.

> **But seek ye first the kingdom of God, and his righteousness; and *all these things* shall be added unto you.**
> **Matthew 6:33**

Notice *God* adds "all these things." When you effectively do *your part* of first establishing His kingdom, then God will do *His part* and give you "all these things" you need and want for the good life *in abundance!*

Furthermore, you may be surprised to learn that God has a pattern of giving the wealth (or "all these things") of the wicked to His children.

The Wealth of the Wicked

As you add to your storehouse of knowledge concerning God's standard operating procedures, you will begin to discover that it is an ongoing, established practice throughout history for God to fulfill the second part of Proverbs 13:22, and transfer the wealth of the wicked to His children at the critical time of their need:

> **. . . and the wealth of the sinner [wicked] is laid up for the just.**
> **Proverbs 13:22**

You know, I can hear you saying, "Brother John, I believe you. I believe you because I believe the Word of God. It says that the wealth of the wicked is laid up for the just, so it must be true, but my logical mind says this is all just too fantastic to be fulfilled. I have to confess that it is beyond my realm of experience. Yes, I believe the Bible, but I must be totally honest. I have never heard of the wealth being turned over to the righteous. I see from my experience that lost, wicked men simply do not give away their wealth."

Please be at ease. *You have heard of this happening* time and time again. Let me now bring some of these times back to your remembrance.

Wealth Given to Abram

How about Abram and the Egyptians? Do you remember that account in the twelfth chapter of Genesis? Abram received great wealth from the wicked Egyptians.

Keep in mind that Abram was flat broke when he arrived in Egypt. Although he came from rich ancestors, when he arrived in Egypt, he definitely was not rich. He couldn't even afford to hire a bodyguard. So, he told his wife, Sarai, to tell everyone she met that she was his sister.

Well, you know the story. Pharaoh fell in love with Sarai, and stated that he would marry her on a certain date. The Scripture says:

> **And he [the Pharaoh] entreated Abram well for her sake: and he had sheep, and oxen, and he asses, and menservants, and maidservants, and she asses, and camels.**
> **Genesis 12:16**

This was all well and good until the Pharaoh discovered Sarai was really Abram's wife. The Pharaoh became so angry that he threw Abram out of Egypt. Note a very interesting point: Pharaoh let Abram keep all of the wealth he had given him!

> **And Pharaoh commanded his men concerning him: and they sent him away, and his wife, and *all that he had.***
> **Genesis 12:20**

In one short visit to Egypt, the wealth of the wicked was quickly transferred to the just man, Abram.

Notice how much wealth Abram acquired in this short time. Upon his departure from Egypt he had great substance:

> **And Abram was *very rich in cattle, in silver, and in gold.***
> **Genesis 13:2**

God sent Abram, who a short time before had been poor, out of Egypt with an abundance of cattle, silver, and gold! Abram was *given* the wealth of wicked Egypt.

Further along in this passage, we see that Abram and Lot had acquired *so many possessions* while in Egypt that:

> **... the land was not able to bear them.**
> **Genesis 13:6**

They actually had such great substance that they could not dwell together, for they needed large amounts of land to contain and sustain their large herds.

A close examination of Scripture seems to show that Lot's wealth came from his association with Abram. It is important to notice this fact. Abram's wealth was so excessive that even his nephew was able to prosper from his abundance.

Clearly, this shows that when God distributes the wealth, He doesn't mind if His children have more than enough. Listen to what He told Abram:

> . . . **Lift up now thine eyes, and look from the place where thou art northward, and southward, and eastward, and westward:**
> **For all the land which thou seest, to thee will I give it, and to thy seed for ever.**
> **Genesis 13:14,15**

These are not the promises of a God who wants His children to dwell in poverty, starvation, and ignorance! No, indeed! The God of Abram *is the God of abundance!*

> **Arise [Abram], walk through the land in the length of it and in the breadth of it; for I will give it unto thee.**
> **Genesis 13:17**

That is not a God who wants His people barely to make it! He gave Abram *more than enough!*

As you study God's Word carefully, you will find that God has clearly stated His intention to take very good care of His children, especially those who walk in His footsteps and obey His will.

Also, keep in mind that God gave all of this land to Abram and his seed (the righteous). Remember that every bit of this property was once owned by wicked, heathen men, and God gave it to the just. The wealth of the wicked *is* laid up for the just.

Wealth Given to Isaac

Let's now look at another case where the wealth of the wicked was transferred to the just. Observe this process as it operated in the life of Isaac. He, too, experienced the God-ordained transfer of the wealth of the wicked into his possession.

While Isaac was living in his homeland, he ran out of supplies because of a harsh famine, so he decided to do as his father before him had done, and go down into Egypt.

Isaac got as far as the land of the Philistines when God told him to stop. He told Isaac to stay out of Egypt, and to continue dwelling in the land of the wicked Philistines, a land that the famine had rendered barren and seemingly non-productive. Yet God promised Isaac that if he followed His instructions (instructions you and I would probably label as "foolish"), he would prosper.

> **Sojourn in this land, and I will be with thee, and will bless thee; for unto thee, and unto thy seed, I will give all these countries, and I will perform the oath which I swore unto Abraham thy father.**
> **Genesis 26:3**

Some will read this passage and immediately assume that God meant an abundance of *spiritual blessings.* Oh, how we love to give our own definition to God's Word. See what God means by *blessings* in the midst of a famine.

> **Then Isaac sowed in that land [a land in the midst of famine], and received in the same year an hundredfold: and the Lord blessed him.**
> **Genesis 26:12**

In verse 14, we see a further inventory of what God had given to Isaac.

> **For he had possession of** *flocks,* **and
> possession of** *herds,* **and great** *store of servants:*
> *and the Philistines envied him.*
> **Genesis 26:14**

Are we to believe the Philistines envied Isaac's spiritual heritage? Are we to believe they envied Isaac's good standing with God? *Of course not!* The Philistines envied Isaac because he had huge crops for food in the midst of famine, crops he was able to sell for huge amounts of money to buy large flocks of sheep for meat and for clothing, and because he had a "great store" of servants to wait on his every need. In the midst of famine, Isaac cleaned out the wealth of the Philistines.

That's why the Philistines envied Isaac! He was the son of a living God who prospers His sons and daughters by giving them the wealth of the wicked.

Yes, of course Isaac first and foremost had a deep *spiritual inheritance,* but God had also earmarked an abundant *material, earthly inheritance* for him, just as He had for Abram.

That's the same thing He wants for you:

> **Every man also to whom God hath given
> riches and wealth, and hath given him power to
> eat thereof, and to** *take his portion,* **and to rejoice
> in his labor;** *this is the gift of God.*
> **Ecclesiastes 5:19**

God gives both *spiritual and financial* wealth to His people. Poverty is simply not a biblical principle. It is time for the obedient and industrious saints of God to stop claiming that poverty is what God wants for their lives!

Friend, let's face it, *poverty is not God's perfect will for you.* To live daily on the brink of insufficiency and claim that it is God's intended status for you is a spiritual mistake. In biblical illustration after illustration, the same truth keeps emerging: God has a people, and God takes care of His people in *the spiritual, the physical,* and *the financial realms.*

Hear the beloved Apostle John declare it:

> **Beloved, I wish above all things that thou mayest *prosper* and *be in health,* even *as thy soul prospereth.***
>
> **3 John 2**

Wealth Given to Jacob

In the thirty-first chapter of Genesis, we *once again* see this principle of taking the wealth of the wicked and giving it to the just, illustrated in the life of Jacob. If you are plagued by a crooked or unsympathetic boss whom you believe hinders God's ability to flow His abundance into your life, then read this next section closely!

No one had a more crooked, stingy, unsympathetic boss than Jacob. Laban was crooked, crooked, crooked, and he was a real tightwad! Ten times, Laban changed Jacob's compensation program! Jacob worked seven years to marry Laban's beautiful daughter, only to have Laban secretly switch daughters at the wedding, and trick Jacob into a marriage with his plain daughter.

After Jacob worked faithfully for Laban for many years, God instructed him to "return to the land of thy fathers." Naturally, Jacob was willing to obey.

Before he left, Jacob revealed to his wives God's amazing, divine principle of taking the wealth of the wicked and giving it to the just, the principle that had been operating in his life as he had worked for their father, Laban.

Read these verses carefully, for they provide a major breakthrough to understanding the mind of God, and to destroying any previous conceptions you may have about what God will do for His children.

> **And ye know that with all my power I have served your father.**
> **And your father hath deceived me, and changed my wages ten times;** *but God suffered him not to hurt me.*
> **If he said thus, The speckled shall be thy wages; then all the cattle bare speckled: and if he said thus, The ringstraked shall be thy hire; then bare all the cattle ringstraked.**
> **Thus God** *hath taken away the cattle of your father, and given them to me.*
> **Genesis 31:6-9**

God took the wealth of wicked Laban and gave it to Jacob! Laban could do nothing to stop the transfer of his wealth to Jacob once God started the process. When Laban said he would pay Jacob only in the speckled cattle, God made all the cattle have speckled young. When Laban said he would pay only in striped cattle, then God made all the calves striped.

God took the wealth of wicked Laban and gave it to righteous Jacob. The God of Jacob yesterday is the very same God you serve today and your children will serve tomorrow.

The groundwork had already been laid for the Lord's abundance in Jacob's life. The Scripture says:

> **And Jacob vowed a vow, saying, If God will be with me, and will keep me in this way that I go, and will give me bread to eat, and raiment to put on,**
>
> **So that I come again to my father's house in peace; then shall the Lord be my God:**
>
> **And this stone, which I have set for a pillar, shall be God's house: and of all that thou shalt give me I will surely *give* the tenth unto thee.**
>
> **Genesis 28:20-22**

Jacob clearly covenanted with God that if He would bless him, then surely he (Jacob) would give a tenth of all he received to God.

Many people construe this vow to mean that Jacob would then begin to tithe, but that simply is not the case. In the Book of Hebrews, we see that Israel (Jacob's new name) had tithed in the loins of Abraham.

> **And verily they that are of the sons of Levi, who receive the office of the priesthood, have a commandment to *take* tithes of the people according to the law, that is, of their brethren, though they come out of the loins of Abraham.**
>
> **Hebrews 7:5**

All of the seed of Abraham were already tithers. Jacob's promise to God was not that he would become a tither after God blessed him—he was already tithing! Remember, Jacob was the one of Isaac's sons who sought after the things of God. Surely, he was a tither from his early years.

Jacob told God he would *give* Him 10 percent. The tithe is not something we *give* to God; it is something we owe to God, for it is *His* to take.

> **And all the tithe of the land, whether of the seed of the land, or of the fruit of the tree, is the Lord's: it is holy unto the Lord.**
> **Leviticus 27:30**

Jacob was vowing with God to *give* him 10 percent *over and above* his tithe, in appreciation for the abundant blessings of God. He established a generous measure of return from God by the generous measure of the offerings he gave to God over and above the tithe. Immediately, because Jacob's faithful tithe had already opened the windows of heaven to him, God poured out a blessing to him according to the measure of his abundant offering. Jacob's offering, not his tithe, determined the amount God returned to him:

> **Give, and it shall be given unto you; good measure, pressed down, and shaken together, and running over, shall men give into your bosom. *For with the same measure that ye mete withal it shall be measured to you again.***
> **Luke 6:38**

The Bible says it happened to Abram! It happened to Isaac! It happened to Jacob! Each one of these great men of God saw the wealth (hard assets) of the wicked transferred from the wicked and placed into his hands.

Wealth Given to Christians

The same amazing process happened again right at the beginning of the Christian era. Do you know when, in the last 1900 years, God took the greatest amount of the wealth of the wicked and gave it to His sons and daughters to spread the gospel throughout the entire world?

It happened during the reign of Constantine the Great, ruler of both the eastern and western Roman Empires from 312 to 337 A.D. In the early part of his life, Constantine slaughtered Christians and fed them to the lions. Surely he qualified as a wicked man at the helm of a very wicked nation.

Yet one day God, in His grace, gave this ruthless murderer a vision in the sky, and instructed him to go and conquer in the name of God. Virtually overnight the greater part of the world entered into Christianity. Virtually overnight the great *wealth of the Roman Empire started to flow into the hands of the Christians.* Maybe it was not the on-fire Christianity of the early apostles, but God still gave the wealth of the wicked to His children!

In 313 A.D., Constantine issued a law that changed the course of human history, the Edict of Milan, which for the first time legalized Christianity in the Roman Empire. *All* the power of Rome suddenly became the *power of the Church!* The wealth and resources of the Roman Empire were now at the disposal of the Church. Every part of the known world was touched by this *new doctrine* of Jesus Christ and His willingness to save sinners.

You will be glad to know that on his deathbed, in 337 A.D., Constantine himself finally became a Christian!

Now, notice carefully that with the transfer of the wealth of the Roman Empire to Christianity, the objection of many well-meaning critics of this message is put to rest. They say, "These scriptures of the transfer of the wealth of the wicked are purely Old Testament, and do not apply to New Testament times."

I leave the decision up to you. Is 313 A.D. New Testament times or not? Surely it is, and with this great event, this concept jumps the boundary between Old and New Testaments, and brings this truth right into our day. Remember, God is the same throughout history, yesterday, today, and forever!

The Chosen People Take Egypt's Wealth

Before I end this chapter, let me highlight one, final, powerful example of how God took the wealth of the wicked and freely gave it to the just.

Israel was in bondage for 400 years. They were poorer than poor. Then God said, "Let my people go." How could this poverty-ridden nation, without an economic base, ever bring forth the great revelation of God's law as we find it in Exodus, Leviticus, Numbers, and Deuteronomy?

Let's start at the beginning of Exodus, when God decided to release this nation from Egypt's bondage. Egypt, through the Pharaoh, had a hold on Israel that was so tight and so humanly impossible to break, that Scripture refers to Israel's captivity as an iron furnace:

> **But the Lord hath taken you, and brought**
> **you forth out of *the iron furnace.* . . .**
> **Deuteronomy 4:20**

God used Moses as His man for this great transfer of the wealth of the wicked into the hands of the just. Eleven plagues came in successive waves from God. Each one ended with no release for God's people! Keep in mind that none of these judgments came upon any of the children of Israel.

Finally, God moved in what is no doubt the most powerful judgment since the flood of Noah. The twelfth judgment came in on the wings of the dreaded death angel of God, sweeping across Egypt, taking the lives of every firstborn of men and beasts.

Now, on the evening of the greatest of these judgments, God came to Moses with very strange instructions.

> **And the Lord said unto Moses, Yet will I bring one plague more upon Pharaoh, and upon Egypt; afterwards he will let you go hence: when he shall let you go, he shall surely thrust you out hence altogether.**
>
> **Speak now in the ears of the people, and let every man borrow of his neighbor, and every woman of her neighbor, jewels of silver, and jewels of gold.**
>
> **And the Lord gave the people favor in the sight of the Egyptians. . . .**
>
> **Exodus 11:1-3**
>
> **And the children of Israel did according to the word of Moses; and they borrowed of the Egyptians jewels of silver, and jewels of gold, and raiment:**
>
> **And the Lord gave the people favor in the sight of the Egyptians, so that they lent unto them such things as they required. And they spoiled the Egyptians.**
>
> **Exodus 12:35,36**

Are you seeing the miracle here? Egypt was full of the dead firstborn of all living things; there were rivers of blood, lice, and boils everywhere, and here came the unscathed Israelites, asking these bewildered, defeated Egyptians, "By the way, before we leave here, may we please borrow all of your gold and silver and valuables?" The Egyptians *freely gave* all their gold, silver, and other precious possessions.

What a miracle! When Israel came out of bondage, Exodus 12:37 says they numbered about 600,000 men. If you add women and children, probably more than three and a half million Israelites left Egypt, but not as slaves! Three and a half million millionaires headed for the desert, equipped with virtually everything they needed!

Did you ever wonder what possessed the Egyptians to dare to enter the watery, walled canyon that crossed the Red Sea? The Word tells us that the Israelites were so rich, and the Egyptians now so poor, that the wealth of the Israelites tempted the Egyptians to follow them into the parted Red Sea.

> **The enemy said, I will pursue, I will overtake, I will *divide the spoil.* . . .**
> **Exodus 15:9**

The Purpose for the Wealth

After 400 years of poverty, the children of Israel were now rich. They had great wealth. *Let the depth of this truth come forth:* God had given the Israelites the wealth of the wicked of Egypt, and yet, there was absolutely nothing in the wilderness on which to spend that wealth!

They had silver and gold, but there were no stores and no shopping centers. Their clothes never wore out! They never needed to buy food. They had manna and quail to eat, water to drink, and light from the pillar of fire by night.

Now get the *real purpose* that God gave the wealth of the wicked to the children of God. The only thing they could use the gold and silver for was to build the tabernacle in the wilderness!

. . . and I will prepare him an habitation. . . .
Exodus 15:2

God wanted them to take the gold and silver of the wicked, wealthy Egyptians, not to lavish upon themselves, but that they might build Him a dwelling place in their midst.

Please get this point well. *The wealth of Egypt was for building the dwelling place of God.* The value of that great building with its gold, silver, precious wood, jewels, and so on, was astronomical.

You cannot help but notice the parallel of these former days with the last days in which we now dwell. This time, *God is giving us the wealth of the wicked so that we can build Him a temple, a holy habitation not made with hands, but one made with lively stones.* This end-time temple is not a mortar-and-stone building. *It is the Church* of the Lord Jesus Christ, made of human bodies of the redeemed who are the true temple of the living God, the dwelling place of God Jehovah.

In the next chapter, we'll take a closer look at the one who would deny us God's bounty. Can he do it? *Only if we let him!*

2

The Liar

This chapter is about the most successful thief and liar in the history of the universe, and how you can combat him. He is a deceptive, calculating plunderer who has moved freely in and out of our lives. Every individual on the face of this planet has been in some way defrauded or robbed by him.

In the United States alone, he has stolen the joys of family life from millions. He has sold his destructive doctrine of *a better life through divorce* to one out of two marriages. Single parents now struggle daily in a desperate drive to survive after the sudden and ugly shock of family separation. They blame infidelity, irreconcilable differences, and circumstances beyond their control, never naming the real culprit; so the thief continues to escape trial, roaming free to rob again!

His methods include many different forms of robbery. He steals countless children from Christian homes by his seductive temptations to sin. He eases their stress by offering them drugs. He releases their sexual frustrations by involving them in premarital sex. He even solves their sense of isolation and rejection by offering them homosexuality.

This thief also steals the actual physical possessions of millions of Christians everywhere. He has *ripped off* from God's children the quality of life God intended for them. Much of the inheritance of the saints is now locked away in his treasure chest, financing the kingdom of darkness instead of the kingdom of light.

You Have Been Ripped Off

Some of you may think I choose the term *ripped off* because I am trying to use modern language to describe a theft. My choice of words has nothing to do with modern language!

When someone walks into your house, sticks a loaded gun in your face, ties you up with a rough cord, begins to load his van with your goods, and then smugly walks out your front door, that is not mere robbery. I am sorry, but robbery is too polite a term! You have been ripped off!

Theft is a painful, ripping sensation that hurts down to the core of your being. It is a personal violation of your private life. When you are deprived by any means of something of value that is lawfully yours, then make no mistake about it, you have been ripped off!

By now, you might be saying, "Brother John, what does all of this talk about robbery and being ripped off have to do with me? I've never been robbed."

Well, I've never met a Christian who hasn't been victimized by this thief. He has performed his destructive deeds, taking from the saints of God what is rightfully theirs, in virtually every Christian life I have ever known.

I will not hold you in suspense any longer. No doubt you have already guessed who that master criminal is. He is the devil. He has taken more loot in his reign of terror than ever imagined. Billions of dollars have been stolen from the children of God as they have marched on this planet in the last two thousand years.

These robberies occur everywhere you look. How many Christians have made what looked to be a good investment, only to watch it go bad? How many have gone off on their own to form some sort of new company or business, only to see it fail?

Hundreds of times I have heard confused wives confess to me, "I don't know what happened. When my husband started his own business, we were sure it would be a success. He had a good working knowledge of his product, and there seemed to be strong demand, but the minute he hung out the company sign, things started going wrong."

In counseling, my wife and I have many times had to help piece back together families shattered by this type of trauma. Time and time again we hear, "We had a beautiful home in a lovely community, and Bill had a good job, but we felt the Lord was leading us to go to another place. So, we sold our house, Bill quit his job, and we went, in faith."

You know the rest of the story, because you have heard it before. You may have even lived it. "Well, Brother John, we just don't know what happened. One thing after another went wrong. Bill could not find work. We used up our house money. Our ministry never got off the ground. Now we are broke. We are 32 (or 42, 52, 62, or 72 years old), and we are broke. What happened?"

We have sat for many long hours counseling dear, precious, Christian families who have lost all of their physical possessions — homes, boats, cars — in the name of the Lord! Step by step, Pat and I have had to take them through their painful experiences and begin to show them where in their lives they accepted some deception or lie from the enemy.

God Is Not a Robber

So often, we hear from these dedicated Christians something like, "Maybe God wanted us to lose all of our physical possessions so that we could learn to trust totally in Him." *That is a lie of Satan!*

God would never rip off the possessions of one of His beloved children just to make a point! A careful study of these situations always reveals some sin, or some lie of Satan that is allowed to sneak into the family, opening the door for him to rip off what God had in store for them.

I believe it is time to serve notice on Satan. He has robbed Christians long enough! For too long and in too many situations, he has ripped off our possessions, indiscriminately raped and plundered the saints of God, diminished their quality of life, and taken the lion's share of our assets and possessions from us.

It is time to take a stand. I want you to begin using the Word of God to stop Satan's robbery in your life. It is time to say, "I'm mad at the devil, and I'm not gonna take it any more!" It is time to start taking back what Satan has stolen from you!

There will be no moving into the next dimension God has for His Church until the saints of God know they have dominion over Satan and can *take back, reclaim, lay hold of, and restore* what the devil has taken from them!

All those possessions he has stolen from you can be restored. All those crooked parts in your family relationships can be made straight. All those business and personal rip-offs you have experienced can be reclaimed. However, you must *first understand how the devil works.*

Understand Your Enemy

Satan uses *deception* as his main weapon against you. As you grow to understand your enemy better, you will not only be able to protect yourself from future attacks, but you will also be able to go before God's judicial bar and *reclaim* the victory in battles you have already lost! Along with those victories, you can reclaim those precious possessions that were lost to the enemy.

When you can determine the method of operation of your enemy and what his plans for attack will be, you can destroy his power over you. Look at these verses closely:

> **And then shall that Wicked be revealed, whom the Lord shall consume with the spirit of his mouth, and shall destroy with the brightness of his coming:**
> **Even him, whose coming is after the working of Satan with all power and signs and lying wonders.**
> **2 Thessalonians 2:8,9**

These verses give the first key to understanding your adversary, but you must be careful here. A great part of the truth is hidden from view because of the translation.

Now notice that all through the New Testament, the Greek word *kai* is translated *and,* but it can also mean *even.* The passage translated "and signs and lying wonders" by the King James translators can also be translated *"even* signs, *even* lying wonders," and properly should be in this case.

Further, the proper translation of "Satan with all power" is better rendered "with all the power Satan has."

Let me paraphrase these verses for you: And then shall that Wicked one be revealed whom the Lord shall consume with the Spirit of His mouth, and shall destroy with the brightness of His coming, even him whose coming is after the working of Satan with *all the power Satan has, even [kai] signs, even [kai] lying wonders* [not true wonders, but deceptions].

Are you catching it? *All the power Satan has* is his ability to deceive. Even his signs and wonders are lies. It is important that you grasp this point. Satan is not the powerful prince of darkness that a quick reading of these verses might suggest. He is limited to his deceptive powers. The primary work of the power of darkness is deception.

Life-Changing Key No. 1

The statement I am about to make is one of the most powerful keys I know to change your life and restore your stolen possessions. If you begin to absorb this biblical fact into your spirit, Satan will remain powerless against you.

The only absolute power left on this earth is the power of God, which now dwells in you and is waiting to burst forth and move in this world, and change it for Jesus!

> **That the God of our Lord Jesus Christ, the Father of glory, may give unto you the spirit of wisdom and revelation in the knowledge of him:**
>
> **The eyes of your understanding being enlightened; that ye may know what is the hope of his calling, and what the riches of the glory of his inheritance in the saints,**
>
> **And what is the exceeding greatness of his power to us-ward who believe, according to the working of his mighty power,**
>
> **Which he wrought in Christ, when he raised him from the dead, and set him at his own right hand in the heavenly places.**
>
> **Ephesians 1:17-20**

The apostle prayed that the Father of glory may give unto *you* the spirit of wisdom and the knowledge of Him, that you may know what is the exceeding greatness of His *power to us* who believe, according to the mighty working of His *power.* Pay attention. God wants our eyes opened to this *greatest of powers He has given us.*

Red China is often referred to as the slumbering giant. I've got news for you. The real slumbering giant is the Church of our Lord and Savior, Jesus Christ! When Christians finally realize who they are in Christ, you watch how quickly the Church will grow into a new, powerful, stirring dimension. The day is upon us when Christians will not have to put up with the things that the saints of God put up with in the past.

It is time to abandon the old, worn out thinking such as "God is putting me through this (whatever problem you have) to get me dependent on Him." Throw it in the garbage can where it belongs. It is time to drop the old pie-in-the-sky, in-the-sweet-by-and-by thinking and replace it with the spiritual rights, the heavenly heritage that goes with being a child of the King — not someday in the future, but right now!

It is time to stop saying, "Oh, Lord, I am not worthy," and start saying, "In the name of Jesus, Satan, I command you to back off! I put you on notice that your past victories over me and my goods are going to cost you dearly!"

This is a new day! The new breed of saint that God is bringing forth in these last days has a way to put the crooked things straight. He has the ability to take back what the devil has taken from him.

Life-Changing Key No. 2

The truth about how to take back your stolen property has been hidden for thousands of years in the Word of God. You have read it over and over, but did not realize you could apply it in your life.

There is a "law of retribution," and it is in God's Word.

You can work this law in your life today, once you know how to apply it. Look first at the Book of Exodus:

> If a man shall steal an ox, or a sheep, and kill it, or sell it; he shall restore five oxen for an ox, and four sheep for a sheep.
> If a thief be found breaking up, and be smitten that he die, there shall no blood be shed for him.
> . . . for he should make full restitution; if he have nothing, then he shall be sold for his theft.
> If the theft be certainly found in *his hand alive,* whether it be ox, or ass, or sheep; *he shall restore double.*
> If a man shall cause a field or vineyard to be eaten, and shall put in his beast, and shall

feed in another man's field; of the best of his own field, and of the best of his own vineyard, shall he make restitution.

If fire break out, and catch in thorns, so that the stacks of corn, or the standing corn, or the field, be consumed therewith; he that kindled the fire shall surely make restitution.

If a man shall deliver unto his neighbor money or stuff to keep, and it be stolen out of the man's house; if the thief be found, let him pay double.

If the thief be not found, then the master of the house shall be brought unto the judges, to see whether he have put his hand unto his neighbor's goods.

For all manner of trespass [*embezzlement* is the literal translation of the Hebrew], whether it be for ox, for ass, for sheep, for raiment, or for any manner of lost thing, which another challengeth to *be his*, the cause of both parties shall come before the judges; and whom the judges shall condemn, *he shall pay double unto his neighbor.*

Exodus 22:1-9

Right now, someone reading this is saying, "Brother John, why are you using an antiquated passage? It's Old Testament, and that had to do with Moses and his bunch. It does not apply to me today. I don't even own a vineyard, and my town won't allow sheep in my backyard."

The Lord never changes.

. . . Till heaven and earth pass, one jot or one tittle shall in no wise pass from the law, till all be fulfilled.

Matthew 5:18

We are told clearly in the New Testament that the things that happened in the Old Testament were done for our instruction until the end of the world comes.

As long as there are still things out there that have been stolen from the saints and not yet returned, the children of God can use these particular verses to claim restitution and snatch them back. Read these verses over and over again. They were true during Old Testament times, and they are true today.

Strange as it may seem, you live in a society where it is often against the law to defend your own property. If you hurt a thief in your own home, in many states you are liable for all of his medical costs, and are subject to being sued in a court of law by the thief himself. Most of the time there is no recourse for the damage suffered by the saints, and we hardly ever hear of restitution.

Praise the Lord, God has an answer for His children if they have been victimized by the devil! Praise God, we look to a much higher court for our justice!

With these powerful truths you are assembling in this study, you can subpoena the devil and bring a proper indictment against him before God. Using the law of retribution, he will be found guilty and *forced to make restitution to you.*

Dear friend, I am praying that as you progress from page to page in this chapter, you are beginning to feel hope spring up over those terrible rip-offs from which it seemed impossible to recover; but now, you see that God always provides an answer from His Word.

The Powder-Puff Lion

Satan is not a roaring lion. Satan wants you to perceive him as a vicious, roaring lion, but that simply is not the truth. Notice carefully, the Word does not say he *is* a roaring lion. The Word says he performs *as* a roaring lion.

> **Be sober, be vigilant; because your adversary the devil, *as* a roaring lion, walketh about, seeking whom he may devour.**
> **1 Peter 5:8**

The only power the devil has is deception. He will manifest himself in your mind with deceptive images of his power, strength, and fierceness.

You may say, "Brother John, Satan has taken things from me. He has destroyed my finances, led my children into lives of sin, and taken away a great job. Don't tell me he doesn't have power!"

Don't misunderstand me. I am not saying just to turn your back on Satan and say, "If you have any power, take your best shot." However, you must realize that what started out as a garden snake in the third chapter of Genesis turned into a dragon in the twelfth chapter of Revelation.

My, how he grew! Who fed him? How did he get so strong? We gave him power by bragging on how strong he is. Remember, the saints shall have whatsoever they say.

> **For verily I say unto you, That whosoever shall say unto this mountain, Be thou removed, and be thou cast into the sea; and shall not doubt in his heart, but shall believe that those things**

**which he saith shall come to pass; he shall have
whatsoever he saith.**
Mark 11:23

The saints have breathed power into the devil over the last 2,000 years. This new power gives him the ability to do some real damage to the uninformed children of God; *but, the Word tells us we can put our foot on him and hold him!* We can hold him in check, in the name of Jesus.

And the God of peace shall bruise Satan
under your feet **shortly. . . .**
Romans 16:20

We need to let our precious brothers and sisters know that the devil is *not the roaring lion* they think he is. *It is time for Satan to be defused, defanged, and defeated!* All he is able to do is deceive.

The Thief of John 10:10

Look at the following verse. There is a serious mistake currently being made in the teaching of this scripture.

**The thief cometh not, but for to steal, and to
kill, and to destroy: I am come that they might
have life, and that they might have it more
abundantly.**
John 10:10

The very teachers who are attempting to defuse the power of the devil are unwittingly feeding him power by teaching that the thief of John 10:10 is the devil.

If the thief in John 10:10 is the devil, then he *does* have the power to steal, to kill, and to destroy, *but this scripture is not talking about Satan!*

All over our land, good, godly men are giving Satan power by attributing to him the power of John 10:10. As they speak that he has destructive power, the devil receives destructive power over those saints who believe it. As they speak that he has the power to steal, the devil receives stealing power. As they speak that he has the power to kill, the devil receives the power to take lives.

Why? *because the power over life and death is in your mouth!*

> **Death and life are in the power of the tongue. . . .**
> **Proverbs 18:21**

If you read John 10:10 in the complete context, a totally different picture emerges. The context of this verse deals with false teachers, false prophets, and false shepherds who were among the sheep, and these teachers and prophets and shepherds were the ones killing, stealing, robbing, and destroying!

If you look closely, you will find the devil is described in John 10:10-12, not as a thief, but as the wolf. He is the wolf that the hireling shepherd was supposed to watch for in order to warn the sheep, but the hireling shepherd left the sheep and fled the scene. The devil is not the thief spoken of in this verse!

One of the reasons we have a planet racked with death today, after immortality has been purchased for us by Jesus Christ (2 Timothy 1:10), is that our teachers and prophets and shepherds have been giving strength to the devil by teaching us of his power, instead of about the power God has given us over him.

> **Behold,** *I give unto you power* **to tread on serpents and scorpions, and** *over all the power* **of the enemy: and nothing shall by any means hurt you.**
> **Luke 10:19**

We have heard about death until it is so much ingrained in us that on a certain day, we just die.

You see, when you operate in the human mind, you can create whatever illusion you put into it. It will faithfully reproduce a thought, and put that thought into the real world where you walk.

The thieves, killers, and destroyers have not been Satan, but you and I have handed our power over to him by listening to and believing incorrect teachings on this particular scripture.

If you believe Satan can kill you, he will. If you believe he can rob you, he will. If you believe he can destroy you, he will.

Satan does not have the power to take your life. There are only six ways people on this planet die:

1. By their own hands
2. By the hands of another
3. By fearing death (Job 3:25)
4. By breaking natural laws
5. By succumbing to the aging process
6. By sickness or disease

Look at the following scriptures, and as you read them, bear in mind that these verses are further proof that John 10:10 is not speaking of Satan.

> **Forasmuch then as the children are**
> **partakers of flesh and blood, he also himself**
> **likewise took part of the same; that through**
> **death he might destroy him that** *had* **the power of**
> **death, that is, the devil;**
> **And deliver them who through** *fear of death*
> **were all their lifetime subject to bondage.**
> **Hebrews 2:14,15**

Are you understanding what the Word of God is saying? The power of death has been taken from Satan. When the children of God rise up in the knowledge of who they are and what they are, and who the devil is and what he is not, then the devil will be forever under our feet.

We must take dominion over this world, over death, over our environment, and over our circumstances if we are going to rule in the name of the King of Kings and Lord of Lords. Do you think Jesus is coming back to this earth to reign with a group of Satan-dominated, fearful, and defeated saints? Remember, He is coming to rule *with* us, not *for* us (2 Timothy 2:12).

Read the context of the following verses:

> **All that ever came before me are thieves and**
> **robbers: but the sheep did not hear them.**
> **I am the door: by me if any man enter in, he**
> **shall be saved, and shall go in and out, and find**
> **pasture.**
> **The thief cometh not, but for to steal. . . .**
> **John 10:8-10**

This passage is not talking about Satan! True, there are places in Scripture where Satan is described as a thief. If you do your own independent study of these scriptures, you will find that the only thing Satan can steal from you in his own power is the Word of God. I do not intend to minimize that theft one bit. If he can steal the Word of God from you, he can steal all of your power over him, and he can easily take command of your possessions.

Your strength over Satan rests in what the Word says. If you live in the Word, *you live in power!* If you live in the Word, *you rule — Satan serves!*

If you allow him to steal the Word, *you live in defeat! You serve — Satan rules!*

Satan has the ability to steal the Word, if you allow it, so he is indeed a thief in that respect. However, you need to be careful about the biblical concept of thieves. The Bible even likens our Lord to a thief: it teaches He will come "as a thief in the night" (1 Thessalonians 5:2).

You need to be very careful in your understanding about any power you attribute to Satan. He has the power to steal from us only if we give it to him. By himself, he has no power. *Satan is only a powder-puff lion!*

A Defeated Foe

I used to embellish the devil with undeserved power. A friend of mine would die, and I would say, "Well, the devil killed him." Each time I did that, I would pour more gunpowder into the devil's ammunition dump.

Why go around kicking a dead dog? You can kick a dead dog, and he will move. However, *he moves only by the power of your kick!*

Satan is like a dead dog. He is defeated. Every time we acknowledge his power over us, we kick him, and he moves. He absorbs our energy, and it moves him. The battle cannot continue if you stop kicking life into him. Saint of God, wake up! The foe is defeated!

You must learn that when you give something attention, you give it strength. In my younger days, I used to get in more fights with the devil. Man, I'd fight those demons up and down the platform. I would fight them in the homes of my congregation and out on the city streets.

Now God has shown me a better way. One day a fellow came down the aisle of my church, escorted by his mother. When he got in front of me, he started slobbering and acting like a mad dog. I just shut my microphone off, looked squarely into his dazed eyes, and with the authority of Jesus declared, *"In the name of Jesus, you shut your mouth and don't you say another word!"* I refused to give the demon attention, and immediately, he was quiet.

When you give something attention, you give it strength. You give Satan power when you constantly acknowledge his presence. Quit letting him run your life. Satan is defeated and absolutely powerless.

Do you understand what I am saying? How foolish it is for us to get this vision in our minds that the devil is so strong! Any time you give strength to a defeated foe, you are making a serious mistake.

Let's look at another stunning example from God's Word of the defeated state of Satan. The Scripture here is talking about the appearing of the Holy Ghost:

> **And when he is come, he will reprove [convince] the world of sin, and of righteousness, and of judgment:**

Of sin, because they believe not on me;
Of righteousness, because I go to my Father,
and ye see me no more;
Of judgment, because *the prince of this world*
is judged.

John 16:8-11

In the Greek lexicon, the word *judged* means "to separate or put asunder." To put asunder means to "break in pieces." Now, that's not the fifth, sixth, or seventh definition of the word. That is the *first and primary definition!* Satan is broken into pieces!

The Holy Ghost has come to convince us that Satan, the prince of this world, *is broken into pieces,* while well-meaning but mistaken teachers are trying to convince us that Satan is a killer and thief and possessor of great powers.

Read from John 16:8 right on through to the end of the Bible, and you will never read another word about God judging the devil, until an angel with a big chain and a key in one hand, puts him into the bottomless pit.

One angel handles this supposedly terrible, powerful lion that has been after the Church for the past 2,000 years!

There is not one more thing God needs to do to the devil. There is not a move left that God needs to make against him. The Scripture teaches that the devil will be cast out of the heavenlies by a group of angels, mere messengers for God (Revelation 12:7-9). Actually, if you can believe it, you can cast Satan out of your life right now, and be rid of his interference in your affairs today.

He's a defeated foe! He's destroyed. The Word of God tells us *he's broken into pieces.* He is so weak that one angel, using only one hand, can cast him into the bottomless pit!

How in the world can we be so deceived as to think that this poor, pathetic, defeated enemy of God can rise up in any power, other than the power we give him through our own fear and our own foolish words?

If we really understood the devil's power, we would understand that it was taken from him on Calvary, and that he is *powerless.* Yes, if we really understood the powers of darkness, we would know that they *must bow to the powers of Light,* and we would immediately storm the strongholds of hell and take the world for Jesus!

He roams the planet "as a roaring lion . . . seeking whom he *may* devour" (1 Peter 5:8). You see, he must be granted permission *before he has the power to devour you.* Yes, you must first let him!

The devil does not have any other power except in lying signs and wonders operating through deception in your mind, *as you let him.* The devil can give you *the idea* that he has strength and power. However, you have the power to cast down that idea.

> **(For the weapons of our warfare are not carnal, but mighty through God to the pulling down of strong holds;)**
> **Casting down imaginations, and every high thing that exalteth itself against the knowledge of God, and bringing into captivity every thought to the obedience of Christ.**
> **2 Corinthians 10:4,5**

Now look at this verse again:

> **Forasmuch then as the children are partakers of flesh and blood, he also himself likewise took part of the same; that through death he might destroy him *that had the power* of death, that is, the devil.**
>
> **Hebrews 2:14**

Look at that carefully. It is *past tense*. He *had* the power of death.

The word *destroy* is translated several ways in the New Testament. It is translated *without effect, made void, made of no effect,* and *abolish.* It is time to stop running in fear from the devil. He is destroyed. The power of death he once had is destroyed. The power of the devil has been wiped out!

> **He that committeth sin is of the devil; for the devil sinneth from the beginning. For this purpose the Son of God was manifested, *that he might destroy the works of the devil.***
>
> **1 John 3:8**

The Greek word for *destroy* is *luo,* and *Strong's Concordance* says it means "to loosen, break up, unloose, melt, or put off."

Know Who You Are

Many folks cannot give up the idea of a strong devil. The problem is that they are more comfortable with a strong devil than a defeated devil, because if the devil is really strong, and they are really weak, when they goof up, they can blame him.

No wonder there is no Kingdom of God on earth. No wonder we are no farther than we are. We have gone all across the world and preached the gospel of salvation, and a good number have been saved. However, we have not yet begun to teach Christians *who they are.* We are preaching the gospel *about* the King (Jesus), but we are not preaching the gospel *of* the Kingdom.

Church, it is time to lay hold of this truth. The primary thrust of the Church's outreach can no longer be only getting people saved. We need to enter into the new dimension of our heritage as sons and daughters of the King. It is a time of getting those we have the privilege of seeing saved, grown up into "the measure of the stature of the fullness of Christ" (Ephesians 4:13). The saints of God must come into the truth of *who they are.*

We have created an army of babes. We now need to raise them up into an army that can go forth in the power of God.

The Battle Is in Your Mind

The truth of the matter is that *the battle is in your mind.* As long as you think Satan is mighty and powerful, he can hurt you.

It is time for Christians to let God take them from a defeated human mentality into an overcoming, God-like mentality. None of these phony concepts about Satan can dwell in your mind when you walk in the mind of Christ.

As you begin to walk in His footsteps and imitate Him, you are transformed into His beautiful image, and the superior God-mind will develop in you and manifest the power of God.

Start walking in belief, not whimpering in unbelief. Put on the entire armor of God. Get out and soar into the heavenlies with the mind of Christ.

The Church of Jesus Christ has accepted the deception of Satan long enough. Now it is time to reclaim what that liar has stolen, and once and for all, walk in the heritage of the King! It's time to stop Satan from stealing from us again.

God's Personal Theft-Protection Policy

To fortify us against invasion by Satan, God has given to each of His children a *spiritual theft-protection policy*. The conditions of this policy are written in the Bible:

> **Put on the whole armor of God, that ye may be able to stand *against the wiles of the devil.***
>
> **For we wrestle not against flesh and blood, but against principalities, against powers, against the rulers of the darkness of this world, against spiritual wickedness in high places.**
>
> **Wherefore take unto you *the whole armor of God,* that ye may be able to withstand in the evil day, and having done all, to stand.**
>
> **Stand therefore, having your loins girt about with *truth,* and having on the breastplate of *righteousness;***
>
> **And your feet shod with the preparation of the gospel of *peace;***
>
> **Above all, taking the shield of *faith,* wherewith ye shall be able to quench all the fiery darts of the wicked.**
>
> **And take the helmet of *salvation,* and the sword of the Spirit, which is the *word of God:***
>
> **Praying always with all prayer and supplication in the Spirit. . . .**
>
> **Ephesians 6:11-18**

You are in a spiritual war! Satan has no power over your life, but you must bring him into containment by skillfully using God's theft-protection policy.

In ourselves, you and I are no match for Satan. However, *in God's strength,* the devil is *no match for us!*

To be shielded from the devil, we must properly utilize the complete, spiritual theft-protection policy God has provided for us. Notice, I said *complete.* God says, "Put on the whole armor of God," not part of it, *but all of it.*

If we follow the conditions of God's policy, we will stand in complete protection, and we will be totally invulnerable to the attacks of the devil.

There are six things God stipulates we must do:

1. Gird your loins with *truth*.

In the world, the battles are fought among large corporations in the courts of law with lies, exaggerations, and evasions of the truth. The entire training of a lawyer centers not around truth, but around the proper protection of his client, even if it means suppression of the truth.

In God's heavenly court system, *truth prevails!* Jesus Himself is Truth.

> **... I am the way, the truth, and the life. ...**
> **John 14:6**

Jesus is Truth, and Satan is deception. The devil himself *is* deception!

> **. . . When he speaketh a lie, he speaketh of
> his own: for he is a liar, and the father of it.**
> **John 8:44**

Your spiritual theft-protection policy demands that you be truthful; lying forfeits the battle to the father of lies. When you lie, the price you pay is that you step out of the provision of God's protection plan. You open the doors to your house and invite Satan to enter and take your energy, strength, and influence.

Truth is the foundation of God's protection plan in your life! Watch your words carefully. Keep your loins wrapped in truth.

Remember, the loins are where the reproduction process takes place. Be sure that what you bring forth is always in accord with God. Always bring forth the truth.

2. Wear the breastplate of *righteousness.*

If you want God's power and protection in your spiritual home, then you must stand before him in *righteousness.*

We have no righteousness except through Jesus Christ.

> **But we are all as an unclean thing, and all
> our righteousnesses are as filthy rags. . . .**
> **Isaiah 64:6**

There is only one way to experience the righteousness of Jesus.

> **If we confess our sins, he is faithful and just
> to forgive us our sins, and to cleanse us from all
> unrighteousness.**
>
> **1 John 1:9**

Satan can use sin to condemn you, overthrow your life, and take your goods. If there is sin in your life, go to Jesus and ask for His forgiveness. Through the forgiveness of Jesus, the devil loses all ability to penetrate your heart through condemnation.

Remember that God can do a quick work in those who walk in righteousness.

> **For he will finish the work, and cut it short
> in righteousness: because a short work will the
> Lord make upon the earth.**
>
> **Romans 9:28**

3. Have your feet shod with the gospel of *peace.*

This passage is often misunderstood, and even skipped. It simply means that we must be willing to witness before the world that Jesus Christ is Lord. The feet are the vehicle Scripture often uses to portray the carrying of God's message to others.

> **How beautiful upon the mountains are the
> feet of him that bringeth good tidings, that
> publisheth peace; that bringeth good tidings of
> good, that publisheth salvation; that saith unto
> Zion, Thy God reigneth!**
>
> **Isaiah 52:7**

Many Christians misunderstand God's command to:

> **. . . Go ye into all the world, and preach the
> gospel to every creature.**
>
> **Mark 16:15**

This command is given to more than the missionaries and the preachers. It applies to *everyone* who knows Jesus, and commands us to tell *everyone* who does not know Jesus that He is the Christ, the Savior of the world.

The lady next door that you take to the grocery market needs to know about the saving grace of Jesus Christ. The boss at work needs to hear about salvation. The person who delivers your morning paper needs to know about the good news of the gospel.

Be ready and prepared to share God's Word with the people He brings into your life! As your *feet* take you from one place to another, and you share the *gospel of peace* with others, you are fulfilling one of God's expectations in His spiritual theft-protection policy.

Let your primary business be the spreading of peace. If you do this, then every step you take will carry out the Royal Ambassador's mission, and it will entitle you to the political immunity of the Kingdom of God.

4. Wear the shield of *faith.*

There are many things we do, believing that our actions will please God. Child of God, I've got news for you. There is one ingredient you must have and exercise; it is a vital key to doing anything to please God!

> **But without faith it is impossible to please him. . . .**
> **Hebrews 11:6**

Faith is crucial to our walk. Faith is the part of our armor that God uses to quench the fiery darts of the devil. It is the weapon that makes us *strong,* that allows us to walk in God's *power!*

> ... And his name *through faith* in his name
> hath made this man *strong,* whom ye see and
> know: yea, the faith which is by him hath given
> him this perfect soundness in the presence of you
> all.
>
> **Acts 3:16**

There are so many current, detailed teachings of faith that I will not try to recount them here. However, I recommend that if you have not already done so, you should perform a complete study on faith. Such a study is vital to your Christian growth.

The Word of God names faith as the key to overcoming the circumstances and problems of the world.

> For whatsoever is born of God overcometh
> the world: and this is the victory that overcometh
> the world, *even our faith.*
>
> **1 John 5:4**

5. Wear the helmet of *salvation.*

Salvation is more than a few words uttered by non-believers when they accept Christ Jesus into their hearts. Salvation is a daily walk, a daily yielding to the Spirit of God. Walking in His will demands that your mind becomes the very mind of God.

Football players wear helmets for protection. No matter how severe the impact from a tackle, the helmet acts to absorb the shock so that the player can continue as if the impact had never happened.

So it is when we wear the helmet of salvation. Satan can attempt to assault our lives, but as we walk in the living, daily salvation of Jesus Christ, we can continue as though the lies and deceptions of the enemy never happened!

Remember, the only power Satan has is the power you give him when you accept his deception. *The spiritual battlefield is in the mind!* So the helmet of salvation, the helmet that protects the mind from the devil, is specially vital to your success in life. Through the salvation of Jesus Christ, you and I can echo the powerful words Jesus used when he admonished the devil:

> **And Jesus answered and said unto him, Get thee behind me, Satan: for it is written, Thou shalt worship the Lord thy God, and him only shalt thou serve.**
> **Luke 4:8**

6. Utilize the *Word of God.*

No true soldier would ever go into a battle unarmed. Any enemy would delight in such foolishness and emerge from the confrontation victorious. Yet, so many Christians try to wage spiritual warfare and do not even carry the weapon God has given to them, *His Word.*

The Word of God is a mighty offensive weapon that cuts down every deception and every lie Satan would feed you.

> **No weapon that is formed against thee shall prosper; and every tongue that shall rise against thee in judgment thou shalt condemn. This is the heritage of the servants of the Lord, and their righteousness is of me, saith the Lord.**
> **Isaiah 54:17**

I have had five-year-olds in my congregation who could recite the latest television hamburger commercial, word for word, yet their parents never asked them to memorize one verse of Scripture. I know adults who can quote stock market prices by the hour, yet never memorized one verse of Scripture. How can you fight in a spiritual war if you leave your weapon at home?

As for God, his way is perfect: the word of the Lord is tried: he is a buckler to all those that trust in him.
Psalm 18:30

Stock market prices will change each day. Hamburger commercials will come and go, but as the Bible says:

Heaven and earth shall pass away: but my words shall not pass away.
Mark 13:31

"Put on the whole armor of God . . ." and you will "be able to stand" in the evil day (Ephesians 6:11). You can defend yourself and stop the devil cold. Do not allow him ever to steal from you again.

Part II
God's Plan: Tithes, Offerings, and Laws of the Harvest

3
Tithes and Giving

God has always been the greatest giver!

> **For by grace are ye saved through faith; and that not of yourselves:** *it is the gift of God:* **Not of works, lest any man should boast.**
> **Ephesians 2:8,9**

It is God's nature to give. *God the Father freely gives us all things!* Our very salvation is a free gift from God.

> **He that spared not his own Son, but delivered him up for us all, how shall he not with him also** *freely give us all things?*
> **Romans 8:32**

Notice that God wants to give us *all things,* not just spiritual things, but *all things!* That includes money for food, clothes, rent, gas, and even for entertainment.

Nothing was more precious to God than His own Son. If we realize that God did not withhold His own Son, then it is not difficult to understand that God will give us *all* things. If we can focus on the greatest gift, Jesus Christ, and the fact that He has already been given to us, then we can know that no lands, houses, treasures, or any other good thing we need will be withheld from us.

Even the Holy Ghost is freely given to all who ask for Him:

> **If ye then, being evil, know how to give good gifts unto your children: how much more shall your heavenly Father *give the Holy Spirit to them that ask him?***
> **Luke 11:13**

Let this concept sink into your spirit. Our God is a giving God! He desires to give us *all things:*

> **According as his divine power hath given unto us *all things* that pertain unto life and godliness. . . .**
> **2 Peter 1:3**

God is the supreme giver of the universe. He gives to us according to His divine power! He desires that we have all things that pertain to life and godliness. Get that truth into your spirit and force out any thoughts that do not come into conformity with this promise from God!

God Wants You to Be Like Him!

Man was created in the image of God, but Satan changed that image when mankind fell into sin. Those who accept Jesus Christ are restored and brought into the image of God once again. Yes, God wants you to be like Him! He literally envisions you like Himself:

> **. . . as he [Jesus] is, so are we in this world.**
> **1 John 4:17**

You know that God is a giver. Now it is important for you to understand that God wants *you* to be a giver! Jesus constantly urged His disciples to give:

1. He told them to give to all who ask (Luke 6:30).

2. He told them they received freely, and freely they should give (Matthew 10:8).

3. He urged them to give the people food (Luke 9:13).

4. He taught, "Give, and it shall be given unto you. . ." (Luke 6:38).

5. He urged them to give to the poor (Mark 14:7).

Jesus lived a lifestyle of giving. He said:

> **. . . I am come that they might have life, and that they might have it more abundantly.**
> **John 10:10**

Yes, God wants us to be like His Son, Jesus, not just in a future life, but right now, by imitating Him.

You can start by taking hold of His wonderful characteristic of giving. Begin to see yourself as a great giver. The giving of Jesus Christ went into every realm. When He met the depressed, He *gave* them a light heart. When He came across the hungry, He *gave* them food to eat. Finally, He made the ultimate sacrifice: He *gave* His life, so that we could have eternal life!

You may never be called upon to give your life's blood for another person; but you can literally become a giver of everything needed by those around you.

With each act of giving, you will receive back from God. One day, if you continue in faithful giving, you will have enough to give in every way God desires. Remember, you are becoming like God, step by step, from glory to glory.

Give Joyfully, Reap Abundantly

God freely gives His gifts to us. Our salvation comes to us freely. The Holy Spirit is given freely. The gifts of the Spirit are given freely.

God expects from us the same willingness to give freely:

> . . . so let him give; not grudgingly, or of necessity: for *God loveth a cheerful giver.*
> **2 Corinthians 9:7**

The next time you write out a check to your local church or favorite ministry, remember that the Lord desires you to give with a cheerful heart. Sing a sacred song as you write out that check. Think of the joy your money will bring to the lives of those who will be saved or delivered through it. Put a big smile on your face when you drop your next offering into the collection basket.

As you give with your cheerful heart, remember that you must also give abundantly if you want to reap abundantly:

> But this I say, He which soweth sparingly shall reap also sparingly; and he which soweth bountifully shall reap also bountifully.
> **2 Corinthians 9:6**

You may be thinking, "But, Brother John, I don't have a lot to give. I have only a small amount of money that I can give to God's work. I guess that means that I will reap sparingly."

That is not true! Remember the poor widow with the two mites (Mark 12)? Jesus said she gave *more* than all the rich men in the temple. Why? Her offering, in proportion to her income, was a much greater gift than anyone else's! Jesus saw her heart. The poor widow gave bountifully, and God rewarded her bountifully. Remember, with the same measure you give, God will give back to you again.

Keep in mind that it is not the amount of your gift itself, but the amount you give *in proportion* to what you have that determines if your gift is bountiful.

Do not be discouraged if your offerings are not so much as you would like them to be. God looks at your offerings in relation to how much you have left after you give.

Giving Always Results in Receiving

This is a vital principle of biblical economics: *Giving always results in receiving!* You have God's Word on it:

> **Give, and it shall be given unto you;** *good measure, pressed down, and shaken together, and running over,* **shall men give into your bosom. For with the same measure that ye mete [give] withal it shall be measured to you again.**
> **Luke 6:38**

Look closely at these *key points:*

1. God promises to return your gift to you. He says *you will receive* a good measure, literally running over.

2. God says your blessings will come from men. God uses people, and so He has no difficulty blessing you from *unexpected places.* The source God uses isn't important; what is vital is that you understand the biblical principle: when you give, you will receive a return.

3. By the same measure you give, you will receive. Remember, the measure is not *how much* you give, but how much you give *in proportion to your income.* This scripture does not promise that if you give five dollars, you will receive five dollars in return. It says that if you give five dollars and that sum is casual pocket money, you will not receive a big measure in return.

If that five dollars is a critical part of your funds, a precious seed out of your limited resources, then it becomes a great measure in God's eyes, and you will receive a great measure in return from Him.

When you become a giver, you automatically move yourself into the realm of a receiver. There are no exceptions to this rule. However, there are levels of receiving:

> **. . . some thirty, and some sixty, and some an hundred.**
> **Mark 4:8**

The measure you use in giving will determine the measure that will be applied to you in receiving. No matter with what measure your gift is made, when you give to God, you *will* receive a return on your giving.

Do not forget it! *Giving always results in receiving.*

Giving Is Your God-Given Right

Are you beginning to see what a joy and a God-given right it is for you to be a giver?

Look again at Luke 6:38:

> **Give, and it shall be given unto you; good measure, pressed down, and shaken together, and running over, shall men give into your bosom. For with the same measure that ye mete withal it shall be measured to you again.**

This promise is not restricted to any particular group of saints; it is every saint's right to claim it if he or she puts into action God's principle of giving.

He promises to give us back more than we give, and He guarantees this return to all those who give to His work. When I say all, I mean *all!* God declares in His Word that He is no respecter of persons. More than once He promises that we will receive in return *more than we give!*

Do you see what this message is doing to your thinking about giving to God? Giving to Him is not an obligation: it is an *opportunity* to put God's biblical principles into action! It is a chance to begin operating your heavenly checking account according to a principle that contradicts the world: *the more you give away to God's work, the more He will return to you so that you can give to His work again!*

> **Yes, God will give you much so that you can give away much. . . .**
> **2 Corinthians 9:11 TLB**

If the entire Body of Christ began to operate in accordance with this biblical principle, we would witness the abundance Moses experienced in the Book of Exodus. His people were so willing to give to build the sanctuary that Moses finally had to stop the giving.

> . . . Let neither man nor woman make any more work for the offering of the sanctuary. So the people were restrained from bringing.
> For the stuff they had was sufficient for all the work to make it, and *too much.*
> **Exodus 36:6,7**

Begin to grasp your God-given right of giving. Act upon God's promise to return to you more than you give. If you will do so, there will come a day when the abundance of God will literally overtake you. You will have enough money to fulfill your every desire to give to God, with plenty left over to supply everything you need and want.

God's Will for You: More Than Enough

When you give, your gift allows God the opportunity to bless you, to keep His promises, and to give you more than enough. By your faithful obedience in giving your tithes and offerings, you set into motion God's biblical principles of economics. Your precious gifts unleash God's power in several areas of your life.

1. Your gift will prosper you.

> A gift . . . whithersoever it turneth, it prospereth.
> **Proverbs 17:8**

2. Your gift will provide you a place in life, and will bring you before great (godly) men in society.

> **A man's gift maketh room for him, and bringeth him before great men.**
> **Proverbs 18:16**

3. Your gift will even bring you friends.

> **... every man is a friend to him that giveth gifts.**
> **Proverbs 19:6**

This verse does not advocate buying friends with your money. It simply means that your giving sets up a magnetism that draws others to you.

4. Your gift will stop anger that is focused against you:

> **A gift in secret pacifieth anger. ...**
> **Proverbs 21:14**

Just for fun, try this when someone is angry with you: send that person a secret gift and watch his or her anger quiet. Don't ask me how it works, but I have seen it do so again and again.

God cares about *you,* and He ministers to you in many areas when you unleash the biblical process of giving, not only in the area of finances. He also ministers to you spiritually. Being a great giver produces a positive, cooperative atmosphere all around you!

Giving Will Spread the Gospel

If enough Christians grasp the principles of biblical economics and apply them in their lives, every church, mission outreach, and Christian television ministry will have the money to finance the gospel.

Ask God how large your special financial gift should be to your local church, a certain Christian television ministry, or a strong missionary outreach. Whatever God tells you to do, you will have the money to do it when you catch this God-given vision!

Remember, giving is a *key* part of your Christian walk. It is not a separate, non-spiritual act of writing out a check. Giving of your finances to God is a deep, personal interaction with God Himself, and is as much a part of your Christianity as your time of prayer.

So do not just give your money without thought or without prayer. Ask God where you should direct your gifts, and even ask Him how much you should give. God has a definite plan for your finances, and He cares about your individual offerings.

Remember, God is a great giver, and He wants you to be one too.

> How then shall they call on him in whom they have not believed? and how shall they believe in him of whom they have not heard? and how shall they hear without a preacher?
>
> And how shall they preach, except they be sent? ...
>
> **Romans 10:14,15**

I believe there is an answer to this crucial question. They will be sent by those who put God's plan of giving and receiving to work and learn to operate complete dominion over every aspect of their finances!

Because the verses pertaining to finances have not been properly applied over the past 2,000 years, the Church is now weak, anemic, under-financed, and must beg each week for the funds to keep going; then it must spend those hard-earned tithes and offerings on mortgage payments while the world cries for spiritual ministry. That's not what God intended!

Here is the challenge. If you will apply God's principles of biblical economics in your own life, if you will muster the courage to unleash the process by giving, then your finances will be blessed abundantly, and God's Church will begin to grow beyond anything we can imagine.

Ministers will be trained and sent forth, because there will be more than enough money to send them. Television programs will beam the gospel around the world, because there will be more than enough money to buy the air time. Churches will expand to hold the ever-increasing numbers of people attracted by the *new breed of Christian who always has more than enough,* even in the midst of famine!

This strategy is exactly what John had in mind when he expressed his prayer for each of us:

> **Beloved, I wish above all things that thou mayest prosper and be in health, even as thy soul prospereth.**
>
> **3 John 2**

You have two choices: 1) You can hold onto your old, traditional beliefs and continue to struggle from paycheck to paycheck. 2) You can *apply* God's economic principles in your own life, and cheerfully *give in good measure.*

If every person who reads this book will choose the second option, and begin freely and joyfully to give of his finances in good measure, soon preachers and ministries all over the world will be screaming, "Stop! Stop! We have enough! The end-time harvest is now assured!"

First Things First! What Is God's Order?

To understand and apply God's principles of biblical economics so that you can have an active, effective *ministry of giving* to finance the end-time harvest, you must first establish God's proper spiritual order in your life.

God the Father should be first. There is no question about that.

> **Jesus said unto him, Thou shalt love the Lord thy God with all thy heart, and with all thy soul, and with all thy mind.**
> **This is the first and great commandment.**
> **Matthew 22:37,38**

That's conclusive. God should be first. Not a single person in all of Christianity would disagree with that statement.

However, to make any major breakthrough in the spiritual area of finances, your spiritual priorities must be absolutely straight. *God must be first in every aspect of your life,* not just in your passive agreement, but in your daily actions.

God must come before money. If you spend three minutes a day praying and ten hours a day going after more money, then who (or what) is your god?

God must come before your own career. If you spend all of your waking hours concentrating on career moves, taking no time to ask God for His will, then who (or what) is your god?

God must come before your own pleasure. If all of your leisure time is spent pursuing pleasure, reading magazines and watching television, while the Bible gathers dust on the dining room table, then who (or what) is your god?

Yes, God must come even before your precious spouse or children. Your family will assume its proper priority only when God is the head of your household.

God is first!

> **I am the Lord thy God, which have brought thee out of the land of Egypt, out of the house of bondage.**
> **Thou shalt have no other gods before me.**
> **Exodus 20:2,3**

If you want to have an active, effective *ministry of giving,* you must prayerfully and carefully make sure that your priorities are clear and in scriptural order. If any area of your life ranks above God, then repent of that wrong emphasis, and prayerfully put your heart in proper order.

Remember that Jesus Himself put this order into focus in the Book of Matthew:

> **But seek ye first the kingdom of God, and his righteousness; and all these things shall be added unto you.**
> **Matthew 6:33**

This careful ordering of your priorities is the way to bring forth the things you need.

God Is First; Who Is Second?

Like many people, you may get very upset when you find out who should come after God in your list of priorities: you.

That's right. The Bible declares that *you are second:*

> **And the second [commandment] is like unto it, Thou shalt love thy neighbor** *as thyself.*
> **On these two commandments hang all the law and the prophets.**
> **Matthew 22:39,40**

Most of us are pretty good about taking care of ourselves. Each month we manage to make the house and car payments, and to meet most of our needs. We know fairly well how to love ourselves second, but the hard part of the commandment is that we are supposed to love our neighbor in the same way!

We are dedicated to meeting our own needs, but the Word of God says we should meet the needs of the world as well. Our neighbor is every man, woman, boy, and girl in the world, regardless of if he or she is saved or lost.

The Church understands clearly whom to love first: God. Then we love ourselves second. We manage to meet our own needs. If Jesus placed our fellow man in a position equal to our own, then to fulfill that commandment, we must be conscious of our neighbor's specific needs, spiritual, physical, and financial.

To be in the center of God's will, and to avoid blocking any of the good things God has for you, you must have as much concern for the people in the world as you have for yourself. God wants *you to prosper* so that you can help others around you to prosper spiritually, physically, and financially!

If you get these two priorities straight, it won't be long before you will be in the center of God's will, and you will begin to optimize the flow of God's abundance in your life. If all the saints caught this vision, it would be only a short time until we would see the precious people of the world drawn to Jesus.

Notice that our prosperity and our health are linked to our soul's prosperity:

> **Beloved, I wish above all things that thou mayest prosper and be in health, even as thy soul prospereth.**
> **3 John 2**

There is no prosperity for the soul which neglects the two greatest commandments. We must put God first, and ourselves and our neighbor second.

Remember, the one who causes his soul to prosper brings himself material prosperity and health, but the one who sins and rebels is bound for destruction:

> **The soul that sinneth, it shall die. . . .**
> **Ezekiel 18:20**

What About the Church?

I want to ask you another question concerning priorities. Which comes first: your job, your family, or your place of worship?

Opinions differ. Most Christians would probably pick their family, but if we can believe the Word, that is not the right answer.

When Isaac moved to Beersheba to live, the first thing he did was *build an altar for worship:*

> **And *he builded an altar there, and called upon the name of the Lord,* and pitched his tent there: and there Isaac's servants digged a well.**
> **Genesis 26:25**

The second thing Isaac did was *set up the place where his family would live:* he pitched his tent. Now, Isaac was a well digger, so the third thing he did was *supervise the digging of a well.*

Isaac put his place of worship first, his family second, and his profession third.

In order to enjoy God's best, we must put God's priorities in order in our lives. The place where you receive your spiritual meat must have a top priority in your life. It should be your local church.

Since you are now unleashing God's abundant blessings in your life through the power of giving, give top priority to your spiritual storehouse, the place where you receive your spiritual nourishment. Make out your tithe and offering checks first, before you pay even a single bill. Set aside the firstfruits for your God.

Isaac put the place where he worshipped God before his family and job. You should follow that pattern in your life also.

Pay Bills or Tithe First?

To have an active, effective ministry of giving in your life, not only must your priorities concerning God be proper, but your priorities in your giving must be clear.

A major question many Christians ask as they begin to put their financial house in order is, "Do I tithe before or after I pay my bills?"

Many people will pay all of their bills, and then, after all of their financial obligations are met, they will tithe to God out of the remaining money. That may be common practice, but it is not what the Bible teaches:

> . . . thou shalt take of *the first of all the fruit* of the earth, which thou shalt bring of thy land that the Lord thy God giveth thee, and shalt put it in a basket, and shalt go unto the place which the Lord thy God shall choose to place his name there.
> And thou shalt speak and say before the Lord thy God. . . .
> And now, behold, I have brought the *firstfruits* of the land, which thou, O Lord, hast given me. And thou shalt set it before the Lord thy God, and worship before the Lord thy God: . . .
> When thou hast made an end of tithing. . . .
> **Deuteronomy 26:2,5,10,12**

The process of bringing the *firstfruits* to God is called "tithing." God's Word says you should tithe first, before you do anything else with your fruits (finances)!

Now, you may say, "But, Brother John, if I tithe first, I won't have enough to pay my bills."

If you believe that, then you are not believing the tithe will open the windows of heaven to you. You see, tithing establishes a new relationship between you and God. It brings you before the open windows of heaven. Literally, this means the treasure house of God is opened to you. If you put God first, as He says to do, then surely He will bless you.

To break through into abounding finances, you must not listen to the devil on this matter; he would have you become fearful and pay your bills first. As surely as you do, there will usually not be enough left over to tithe, much less to make an additional goodwill offering.

Please be wise enough to see that if you tithe and make offerings after all the bills are paid, you are leaving yourself at the mercy of your bills. With this action, your tithes and offerings are under the control of your bills. However, if you tithe first, and give a generous offering, then your bills become subject to the control of your tithes and offerings.

Remember, Malachi 3:10 and 11 speaks of open windows for the tither and uninterrupted harvests for the one who gives offerings. Always keep your bills in their proper place behind the tithe. Put God's business first, and He will put your business first.

What About Paying the Men of God Who Teach the Word?

The Bible instructs a teacher to teach the entire Word of God, no matter what the situation. Tremendous future blessings depend on how you receive this instruction.

Think about the men and women of God who spiritually bless your life. Think about your pastor, Bible teachers, evangelists, missionaries, television and radio ministers, and all the others who minister to you.

Let the elders that rule well be counted worthy of double honor, especially they who labor in the word and doctrine.

> **For the scripture saith, Thou shalt not muzzle the ox that treadeth out the corn. And, the laborer is worthy of his reward.**
> **1 Timothy 5:17,18**

The laborer (ordinary worker) is worthy of his hire, but those who labor in the Word are worthy of *double pay.*

Elijah understood this principle when he commanded the hungry widow of Zarephath to give her last bit of food to him, the man of God:

> **. . . but make me thereof a little cake *first*, and bring it unto me, and *after* make for thee and for thy son.**
> **1 Kings 17:13**

Elijah told the widow to make the cake for him first, not because he didn't care about her needs, but because he knew that as she provided for the man of God, the Lord would provide for her and her family — and *He did!*

> **And she went and did according to the saying of Elijah: and she, and he, and her house, did eat many days.**
> **And the barrel of meal wasted not [was not used up], neither did the cruse of oil fail. . . .**
> **1 Kings 17:15,16**

The Bible teaches clearly that the men of God who minister to you should receive high priority when you begin to distribute the dollars you put into the gospel.

> **Let him that is taught in the word communicate unto [share with] him that teacheth in all good things.**
> **Galatians 6:6**

The Primary Truth: Giving Goes Before Receiving

I want to emphasize the most elementary priority of all. I almost left it unmentioned, but God said I must surely include it: *Giving always goes before receiving!*

The world would have you believe that first you receive, and then you give. So many times I have heard sincere Christians say, "Oh, Brother John, when I receive a million dollars, I'm going to give a great amount to the work of the Lord! You just watch. I know I will."

Well, strangely, the Bible contradicts that bit of human reasoning. The Bible says a person must be faithful in a little, or he will never be faithful in a lot:

> **He that is faithful in that which is least is faithful also in much: and he that is unjust in the least is unjust also in much.**
> **Luke 16:10**

Waiting for abundance before starting to give will not insure the giving of large gifts. It will actually insure just the opposite. You will not give at all.

First things come first. If you want to receive from God, you must first begin to give. The Bible clearly teaches this principle over and over again. Luke 6:38 says to give first, then it will be given to you. Malachi 3:10 says to tithe first, then God will open the windows of heaven, and pour out a blessing upon you.

Every farmer knows this principle: You must sow before you can reap. You will *never* hear a farmer say, "I'm not going to do any planting just yet. God must first give me a harvest of wheat, *then* I'll plant my seed in the field."

He knows that such a thing simply will not happen. He knows he must first plant seeds, no matter how few he has, and then he will get back a harvest.

Does the Lord give you salvation first, and then you give your heart to Him? Of course not. First, *you give* your heart to Him, and then *He gives* you eternal life.

God's principle of first planting, then reaping, is firmly entrenched in every aspect of life, from Genesis to Revelation, from farming to the propagation of every species. *There is no hope of increase without seeding!*

Remember what Solomon said:

> To every thing there is a season, and a time to every purpose under the heaven:
> A time to be born, and a time to die; *a time to plant, and a time to pluck up that which is planted.*
> **Ecclesiastes 3:1,2**

A Breakthrough in Sowing

The following scripture sets the priority for finances:

> But thou shalt remember the Lord thy God: for it is he that giveth thee power to get wealth, *that he may establish his covenant. . . .*
> **Deuteronomy 8:18**

What is the covenant?

> And I will make of thee a great nation, and I will bless thee, and make thy name great; and *thou shalt be a blessing.*
> **Genesis 12:2**

Yes, God wants to bless you so that you can go forth and fulfill His *second priority:* to love and bless your neighbor as you are loved and blessed yourself. God has given you and me the power to get wealth so that we can preach the gospel throughout the world.

Go boldly beyond being blessed into *being a blessing.* You cannot be a blessing to others until you have personally been blessed by God. Surely now is the time for the Church to violently break out of the poverty cycle. It is time to stop the trickle of financial blessings in our lives, and make some breakthroughs that will properly fund our end-time vision of reaching the world with the gospel.

Along with a knowledge of God's plan for abundance, it takes decisive action. The farmer must first plant seeds. Sometimes he sows in very hard ground, from early morning to late at night in the hot sun, often without lunch. If he wants a great harvest, he must fight to get seed into the ground.

The same is true in your financial walk. Sometimes seed planting is very hard. Circumstances may say, "You cannot afford to give fifty dollars." *Do it anyway.*

Circumstances may say, "You cannot afford to give a specific love gift to your pastor *and* give the offering God has instructed for you to send to some special ministry." *Do it anyway.*

Breakthroughs in sowing (giving) always go before breakthroughs in harvesting (receiving). Remember what the Scripture says:

> **And let us not be weary in well doing: for in due season we shall reap [receive], if we faint not.**
>
> **Galatians 6:9**

Kinds of Giving

The Tithe — Is It Still Necessary?

When you tithe, you are only returning to God what is already His. However, because many people consider tithing to be a type of giving, I'm including it in this section.

There is probably more confusion in the Body of Christ about tithing than any other type of "giving." Yet God is not the author of confusion, and His Word on the tithe is clear:

> *Will a man rob God? Yet ye have robbed me.* But ye say, Wherein have we robbed thee? *In tithes and offerings.*
>
> Ye are cursed with a curse: for ye have robbed me, even this whole nation.
>
> Bring ye all the tithes into the storehouse, that there may be meat [food] in mine house, and prove me now herewith, saith the Lord of hosts, if I will not open [for] you the windows of heaven, and pour you out a blessing, that there shall not be room enough to receive it.
>
> **Malachi 3:8-10**

If you are going to receive the God-kind of prosperity in your life, you must not overlook or underemphasize the basic building blocks of your biblical prosperity plan. It is an absolute necessity that you tithe to get the windows of heaven open. *Tithing is not a biblical option.* The tithe is something you literally owe to God.

Please remember, these are not my thoughts. God says that if we do not tithe, we are committing robbery. He says we owe Him the tithe. The tithe is given, not at our discretion, but *because God commands it.* By faithfully bringing the tithe to Him, we establish our basic honesty and obedience. (Read Leviticus 27:30-33, which clearly shows that the tithe belongs to the Lord.)

However, our offerings are given out of our own generosity. They are totally at our own discretion, and they establish the level of our concern for the things of God:

> **Every one must make up his own mind as to how much he should give. Don't force anyone to give more than he really wants to, for cheerful givers are the ones God prizes. God is able to make it up to you by giving you everything you need and more, so that there will not only be enough for your own needs, but plenty left over to give joyfully to others.**
> **2 Corinthians 9:7,8 TLB**

Remember, you and I are not being generous when we tithe. We are simply obeying God. For the Christian, *tithing is not an option.*

In Hebrews 7:1-10, we see that Abraham paid tithes. He paid them for himself, before the dispensation of the law, and also paid them for Levi, who lived under the dispensation of the law. In fact, Abraham tithed for all posterity—for his natural children (seed) and for the spiritual children (seed) who now live in the dispensation of grace.

> **And if ye be Christ's, then are ye Abraham's seed, and heirs according to the promise.**
> **Galatians 3:29**

The obligation of tithing reaches from the pre-law dispensation, through the dispensation of the law, and now, into the post-law dispensation of grace.

Remember, the windows of heaven are opened by faithful giving of tithes, making the tithe absolutely necessary. Without the windows of heaven open, nothing can flow from God to you.

Where Should the Tithe Be Given?

There is great controversy as to where the tithe should be given. Some say it should go to the local church. Others say teaching ministries should receive it. Still others want the tithe to go strictly for world evangelism.

What I understand to be the biblical answer is found in the third chapter of Malachi. There we see that the tithe goes into *the storehouse.* The context indicates that this storehouse is the place where the meat, the Word of God, is kept and supplied to the saints:

> **Bring ye all the tithes into *the storehouse,*
> that there may be meat in mine house, and prove
> me now herewith, saith the Lord of hosts, if I will
> not open you the windows of heaven, and pour
> you out a blessing, that there shall not be room
> enough to receive it.**
>
> **Malachi 3:10**

Where are you being fed the unadulterated Word of God? This is the question you must answer to determine where to give your tithe. The place you are being spiritually fed should be your local church.

Many saints are sick or otherwise unable to journey to church. Perhaps some of these saints receive their spiritual meat from a Christian television or radio program, or a good ministry to shut-ins. Surely this would be one of the few exceptions to the general rule that the tithe should go to the local church.

Notice another aspect of this verse. God says to tithe, and *prove Him.* God is literally challenging us to put Him to the test in this matter of tithing. He wants the windows of heaven to be open in our lives.

It must be wonderfully clear that *God wants only to bless us!* Yet, He cannot do it through closed windows.

Let's keep up our momentum. We know we must tithe, and we know where we should tithe. So, let's keep putting God to the test by consistently tithing, and we will see the windows of heaven open in our lives.

Remember, the tithe goes to the place where we receive our spiritual meat on a consistent basis. For most of us, it is our local church.

Can There Be Prosperity Without the Tithe?

God wants to build an end-time temple, a holy habitation not made with hands. He must have a great, end-time army of special saints to accomplish His vision. He will give the responsibility of building this great end-time dwelling place to those who have proved faithful in financial matters.

That's not just a fancy idea, but it came to me by revelation after years of studying the Holy Bible. It's totally based upon Scripture.

When King Josiah commissioned workers for the restoration of the temple, he gave the work to those craftsmen who had already proved themselves *faithful* in their *financial transactions:*

> And let them deliver it into the hand of the doers of the work . . . to repair the breaches of the house,
> Unto carpenters, and builders, and masons, and to buy timber and hewn stone to repair the house.
> Howbeit *there was no reckoning made with them of the money that was delivered into their hand, because they dealt faithfully.*
> **2 Kings 22:5-7**

These men were not chosen to partake in this labor because they had *promised* to be faithful. They were chosen because they had already *proved* themselves to be faithful! When it came time for King Josiah to choose who would work in the restoration of the temple, God told him to select these men because they had an established record of *dealing faithfully in their finances.*

God uses people who are faithful in their finances, and tithing is part of that faithfulness.

What did Jesus say to His disciples about faithfulness?

> He that is faithful in that which is least is faithful also in much: and he that is unjust in the least is unjust also in much.
> **Luke 16:10**

If you want to be a part of the next big move of God, don't just get your finances in order temporarily; keep them in order from now on.

Remember 1 Corinthians 4:2:

> **Moreover it is required [not just desired]
> in stewards; that a man be found faithful.**

What Is an Offering?

I am sure by now that you have realized an offering is greatly different from a tithe. The tithe is clearly 10 percent of what has been earned, an amount set by God which is paid to Him as a debt, or as a non-negotiable obligation owed to Him. Failure to pay the tithe is plainly called "robbery" in God's Word.

I know that is frank and to the point, but there is no sense in beating around the bush with the Word of God. He says it, so what can we do other than just believe it and abandon all debate?

An offering — now that's a different matter! An offering is not a specified amount; it is totally discretionary on our part, an amount we freely give to God to establish a rate of return from Him. The amount of our offering establishes the measure by which God will bless us and increase our substance.

> **. . . For with the same measure that ye mete
> [give] withal it shall be measured to you again.**
> **Luke 6:38**

An offering is anything we give over and above our tithe. We are not generous givers in the eyes of God when we tithe — the tithe is simply evidence of honesty. It is simply paying God what we *owe* Him.

When we hear the voice of God leading us to help finance a struggling ministry in the Philippines, or a ministry fighting drug abuse in a certain city, now that is an offering—*a freewill, love offering to our God!*

Who is going to tithe to a Christian home for abused children? The only people receiving meat from this spiritual storehouse would be the abused children in the home, and they do not have the finances to support the institution. So that work, and many more projects in God's Kingdom, survive solely through the freewill offerings of God's prosperous people!

Remember, the principles of biblical economics only start when we tithe. They are set in motion when we give generous offerings. There is a great blessing in offerings, because they determine the measure God uses to give back to us. Furthermore, offerings are always a blessing to the ministries receiving them, since in many cases offerings are God's way of meeting their needs.

Through our tithes and offerings, you and I will move into a dynamic new realm as mature Christians, working *with* God, ministering to the needs of a hurting and needy world:

> **And they went forth, and preached every where, the Lord working with them, and confirming the word with signs following. Amen.**
> **Mark 16:20**

The Hidden Blessing of Giving to World Missions

When you seriously search God's Word, you discover there is a spiritual *gift of giving.* That spiritual gift has many different manifestations. One is the giving of an offering.

Here we will talk about another type of giving: specific giving to world missions.

There is a *special type of blessing* God gives to those who support world missions. Read these key verses in their context:

> **Now ye Philippians know also, that in the beginning of the gospel, when I departed from Macedonia [on a great missionary journey], no church communicated [shared] with me as concerning giving and receiving, but ye only.**
>
> **For even in Thessalonica [one of the mission fields] ye sent once and again unto my necessity.**
>
> **Not because I desire a gift: but I desire fruit that may abound to your account. . . .**
>
> ***But my God shall supply all your need according to his riches in glory by Christ Jesus.***
> **Philippians 4:15-17,19**

The last verse of this passage is often quoted out of context. Well-meaning Christians claim Philippians 4:19 because it sounds desirable. Read the entire passage in its God-given context. This promise is given to an exclusive group, those who faithfully support world missions.

The context here shows that God will supply all the needs of those who are doing what the Philippians were doing, giving to world missions. Notice that Paul did not say God would supply their needs *out of* His riches in glory, but he clearly stated God would supply their needs *according to* His riches in glory.

Now, let him who has an ear hear what the Spirit of God is saying. It will witness to you if you are catching a vision of the mind of God. The promise reads, "But my God shall supply all your need *according to* his riches in glory. . . ." The word *according* speaks of God's blessing in the same *quality* (not quantity) as His own riches in glory!

God provides a way for us to have both abundance and quality. Don't allow evil imaginations to arise in your mind and find fault with this statement. Remember, our Lord Jesus Christ is the one who freely gave *the best wine* to His friends at the marriage supper. He also approved when the *costly oil* was poured over Him. Then when He was crucified, *His coat was of the best quality,* motivating the soldiers to cast lots for it. In the Book of Revelation He is seen standing among the golden candlesticks wearing *a girdle of solid gold.*

God will supply the needs of His faithful partners who evangelize the world, *in accordance with His riches in glory!*

Scripturally Giving to Your Teacher

Every Christian has some special teacher who is vital in his life. There are prophecy teachers, Bible teachers, pastors, evangelists, and so on. There is a continual flow of good teaching available to us each day.

The Bible tells us that if we are receiving a blessing from a teacher, then we should share good things with him.

Let him that is taught in the word communicate unto [share with] him that teacheth in all good things.
Galatians 6:6

This verse says we should take our good things and share them with those who teach His Word.

What a wonderful plan this is! The Lord gives us anointed teachers to bring us His Word. After we learn the Word, we go forth and benefit and prosper from that Word. Then, we share some of that prosperity with our teachers to help meet their needs and fulfill God's Word which says:

> **Thou shalt not muzzle the ox when he treadeth out the corn.**
> **Deuteronomy 25:4**

God has decreed that our teachers should eat freely from the harvest they plant in our spirits.

When you give to your teacher, you unleash God's prosperity even more powerfully in your own life. You give the heavenly Father yet another avenue through which He can bless you.

Now look at the next scripture in Galatians:

> **Be not deceived; God is not mocked: for whatsoever a man soweth, that shall he also reap.**
> **Galatians 6:7**

As you sow a blessing *to* your teacher, you will reap a blessing *from* your teacher and gain an even deeper understanding of God's Word. Bless those who teach you, and God promises He will bless you in return.

Removing the Veil From Malachi 3:10

Because of the importance of this principle, I must reemphasize it. This is one of the most important lessons in this book because it answers a statement frequently made by Christians. "Brother John, I have been faithfully tithing for years, and frankly, I have never received a blessing so great that there was not room enough to receive it!"

Every tithing Christian probably relates to this dilemma.

The spiritual principles that govern the blessings of the tithe are contained in Malachi 3:10:

> **Bring ye all the tithes into the storehouse, that there may be meat in mine house, and prove me now herewith, saith the Lord of hosts, if I will not open you the windows of heaven, and pour you out a blessing, that *there shall* not *be room* enough *to receive it*.**

I have emphasized seven words in this text that are written in italics in the *King James Version*. It is common knowledge that all italicized words in the *King James Version* have been added by the translators to the original text. Here is one of the few big errors in the translation of the authorized version.

These words, *there, shall, be, room, to, receive,* and *it,* are added words, which do not clarify the original text, as italicized words are supposed to do, but in my opinion, actually add a meaning that God did not intend.

The passage should properly read, ". . . and pour you out a blessing, *that not enough.*"[1] You see, tithing only opens the windows of heaven.

---

1   *Please read Malachi 3:10 in the following translations: The Berekeley Version, The Jerusalem Bible, The Douay Version, The New English Bible, and Ferrar Fenton's Version. You will find that none of these say there will be a blessing so great "that there shall not be room enough to receive it."*

If your next door neighbor were stealing from you, you wouldn't leave your windows open. The same is true of God. When we fail to tithe, we are stealing from Him, and *the windows of financial blessing* are shut in our lives!

When we do tithe, God opens the windows of heaven, but remember, the literal meaning of the original text says *that is not enough.* We must then complete the process through offerings to establish the rate of return out of those windows. After we tithe to open the windows, then we put to work Luke 6:38.

The only giving we do is through our offerings, over and above the tithe. These offerings are so critical because they determine how much we receive from God through the windows opened by our tithe.

> **. . . For with the same measure that ye mete [give] withal it shall be measured to you again.**
> **Luke 6:38**

Remember, your tithe opens the windows of heaven, and your offering establishes the measure God will use to give back to you through the open windows.

Abundance Is a Process

The principles of biblical economics require time, study, and understanding if they are to become effective and *powerful* in your life. They are *not an instant prosperity formula.* They demand understanding *and* a new relationship with God.

The gift of your salvation is given freely, but it then takes a constant daily walk to keep your relationship with God growing.

You received the Holy Spirit simply by asking, but if you plan to put all of the gifts and fruit of the Holy Spirit into *powerful practice* in your life, it takes a lifetime of interaction with Him.

The same is true of the biblical principle of giving and receiving. It demands careful study. It demands faithful execution in a systematic, concise manner. Then, after faith and patience have done their work, you inherit the promises (Hebrews 6:12).

You have seen that there are many types of giving. You have learned that the tithe is God's money, entrusted to your keeping. Failing to give it back to Him at the proper time is robbery. Tithing is the *foundational principle of biblical economics* since the windows of heaven cannot be opened to you until you tithe.

You learned that offerings are the key to the measure of your prosperity. Your faithful tithing opens the windows, and your faithful, liberal offerings determine how much God will bless you through the open windows. Giving only a little measure of what you have brings a little measure of blessing through the windows, but a big measure brings forth a big blessing.

You now know that God looks at your heart, not at the dollar amount of your gift. He determines the size (or measure) of your gift by what portion it is of what you have left. If you are giving out of your need, even if it is only one cent, your one penny is a gift of more value than a million dollars given by someone else out of his great abundance!

You have discovered that mission giving unleashes a special promise *just for you!* No other saints can experience prosperity in quite the same way as those who give to missions. Mission-minded saints can look forward to both quantity and quality blessings from God.

Giving is a spiritual gift which you and I learn to use by *application*. It is *not enough* for you to understand everything I've written and shared with you in this chapter, and it is not enough for you to memorize every single scripture I've quoted so far, and then *stand in faith* for your prosperity. To achieve your desired prosperity, to achieve the abundance that will give you the ability to participate effectively in the end-time harvest, *you must faithfully apply these principles* in your everyday life.

These principles make no sense to the world, but they make great sense to God, and they are making more and more sense to you as you receive a whole new mentality on the subject of finances. Your mind is being revolutionized and renovated, and brought into line, precept upon precept, with the Word of God!

4

Harvest

All Truth Is Parallel

God multiplies your money in the same way He multiplies the farmer's seed. The hundredfold, sixtyfold, or thirtyfold increase is not limited to the agricultural harvest. The tremendous multiplication principle of the harvest pertains to the Christian's money in the same way it pertains to the farmer's seed. These are not the words of a man; they are the words of God.

The Apostle Paul clearly makes this parallel in the Book of 2 Corinthians.

> . . . remember this—if you give little, you will get little. A farmer who plants just a few seeds will get only a small crop, but if he plants much, he will reap much.
> 2 Corinthians 9:6 TLB

With this statement, Paul points out that the amount of seed planted directly affects the size of the harvest that will be produced. No one questions that this works on the farm. However, in reading further, it becomes evident that Paul's primary purpose is to teach us how to multiply our money seed. He is showing us that the same thing that happens when the farmer plants his seed happens when we give our money. *We will experience a harvest!* By this we know there is a parallel between giving money into the gospel and planting seed into the ground.

Giving Brings Forth Multiplication

God is able to make it up to you by giving you everything you need and more, so that there will not only be enough for your own needs, but plenty left over to give joyfully to others.
2 Corinthians 9:8 TLB

Traditionally we are taught it is wrong to give finances to God expecting to receive finances back from God. The church has misunderstood God's Word on this subject.

Notice this verse is not teaching that if you give a certain amount of money, you will receive back the same amount you gave. It speaks of giving an amount of money and then *receiving back more money* than was originally given. It says you will receive *"everything you need and more."*

If you sow a hundred dollars into the gospel, you will reap many hundreds of dollars back in a money harvest. There is no question about it; God offers the most liberal of terms. Some of His accounts pay a hundredfold increase, others pay a sixtyfold increase, and yet others pay a thirtyfold increase.

. . . [seed] fell into good ground, and brought forth . . . some an hundredfold, some sixtyfold, some thirtyfold.
Matthew 13:8

It Is God's Responsibility to Make Up What You Give!

Pay attention to this next statement, for an important truth is about to be revealed. When you give your finances to God, *He personally takes the responsibility of making them up to you!*

God is able to make it up to you . . .
2 Corinthians 9:8 TLB

That fact in itself is wonderful, but there is more. God always replaces the amount you have given, *plus* a liberal increase! He gives you back not only enough to meet your own need, but abundantly more than you need.

The greatest benefit of giving to God is that each time you give, you reposition yourself for another harvest. There is no limit to the number of times you are allowed to repeat this process. With each planting of seed, you are promised *"everything you need and more so that [the reason for the surplus] there will not only be enough for your own needs, but plenty left over [not to hoard and stack up, but] to give joyfully to others"* (2 Corinthians 9:8 TLB).

With each cycle of this process, the threefold purpose of the financial harvest is accomplished.

1. The gospel is preached.

2. Your needs are abundantly met.

3. You have plenty left over to give joyfully to others.

You Can Have Something to Give

For God, who gives seed to the farmer to
plant, and later on, good crops to harvest and
eat, *will give you more and more seed to plant* and

> **will make it grow so that you can give away more**
> **and more fruit from your harvest.**
>   *Yes, God will give you much so that you can*
> *give away much ....*
>   **2 Corinthians 9:10,11 TLB**

In almost every church in which I speak, in the seminars I conduct, in letters I receive, I hear the same statement again and again. *"Brother John, God has not provided me with any money to give."*

Please believe me. I do not want to incur anyone's wrath. However, I must be faithful to the Word of God. I am duty bound to challenge this scandalous accusation against our God. *God provides seed to every Christian who is willing to give into the gospel.* Look at the Word of God again.

> . . . **God, who gives seed to the farmer**
> **[sower] to plant, . . .** *will give you more and more*
> *seed to plant ....*
>   **2 Corinthians 9:10 TLB**

I am aware that when the offering plate comes around, many Christians do not have any money to put in it. Please understand, this lack of money does not occur because God is not willing to provide these folks with something to give. The real reason this happens is that they are not sowers. God does not promise to give seed to the Christian. *He promises to give seed to the sower.*

The next time you don't have anything to put in the offering plate, try this. Confess to God that you have not been a sower [giver] in the past, but you want to become one. After confessing this, ask God to forgive you; then ask Him to give you an opportunity to give. If you will pray this from a sincere heart, God will surely let you make it up to Him.

Then write on your offering envelope that you are going to give a certain amount as soon as you have it. When you receive those funds from God, be careful to fulfill your commitment by giving them into the gospel as you promised.

This remedy may seem embarrassing, but it is totally effective. Try it. You may not like it, but I guarantee you it will work!

Seed Faith Is Not New

Throughout Christian circles we are constantly confronted with the subject of planting seed. This section is not written to present the seed-faith principle as a new concept. It is written to bring added illumination to the operation of this truth and to help establish the proper operation of the seed-faith principle in your life.

Seed-faith giving is not only a New Testament doctrine. It finds its roots in the Book of Genesis, where every significant Bible teaching finds its beginning.

Seed faith (faith that a seed will multiply) is the system God depends on to assure the propagation of every life form He created on earth. Everyone knows plant life continues to exist by the seed-faith principle. Even human beings reproduce and multiply according to this principle.

The first recorded promise of a Savior was made to Adam and Eve by the seed-faith principle in the Book of Genesis.

> . . . I will put enmity between thee and the woman, and between thy *seed* and her *seed;* it shall bruise thy head, and thou shalt bruise his heel.
>
> **Genesis 3:15**

This first promise of Jesus, the Messiah, was made by God in the form of a seed-faith promise. The seed of the woman would deliver mankind from the curse.

The Church exists today through the seed-faith principle.

> . . . I will make of thee a great nation, and I will bless thee, and make thy name great; and thou shalt be a blessing:
> And I will bless them that bless thee, and curse him that curseth thee: and in thee shall all families of the earth be blessed.
>
> **Genesis 12:2,3**

> . . . if ye be Christ's, then are ye Abraham's seed, and heirs according to the promise.
>
> **Galatians 3:29**

From this early promise made to Abram came the glorious Church with its ultimate commission to bless all the families of the earth. The promise of the Church has existed through thousands of years by way of the seed-faith principle.

Planting financial seed is the God-ordained way to multiply your money. With this said, I can hear someone saying, *"Brother John, that is not the way my ultra-modern, high-tech bank multiplies money. That seed-faith business is old-fashioned and out of date."*

Rather than arguing about this matter, just read the newspapers. Banks — I mean ultra-modern, high-tech banks — fail almost daily. Keep in mind that this modern banking system has brought the nations of the world to the brink of economic collapse.

God's Harvest Principle Is a Higher Principle

Before you dismiss God's method as being impractical, please realize He does not think as we do.

> . . . **My thoughts are not your thoughts, neither are your ways my ways, saith the Lord. For as the heavens are higher than the earth, so are my ways higher than your ways, and my thoughts than your thoughts.**
> **Isaiah 55:8,9**

If you are so foolish as to consider man's monetary system superior to God's, just remember God's system has *never* failed. Man's systems fail daily. God's ways are superior, for they come to us from His ultimately superior mind. Seeding to a financial harvest is God's idea, not man's. He is the only one who promises that when you give to Him, He will give back to you — some a hundredfold, some sixtyfold, and some thirtyfold.

The farmer cannot multiply his seed by the use of inside information or manipulation. If a harvest is to be experienced, God must perform the miracle of increase inside each seed. God alone is able to multiply your seed into a harvest.

Understanding Farming Is Important to Your Financial Harvest

It is important for believers to have a basic understanding of farming. When I first came into the biblical revelation of multiplying money, I knew almost nothing about farming. I had grown up in the city. My lack of farm knowledge was a continual hindrance to me. I found it difficult to bring forth a successful financial harvest without some basic farming knowledge.

Maybe you are faced with this same problem. You live in the age of astronauts, computer whizzes, and advanced technology; yet the Holy Bible is a book originally written in the language of farmers, using illustrations common to farmers.

Do not misunderstand. Your Bible is not obsolete. It can still answer your every need. People in the high-tech age still eat food that comes from the farm. They continue to be born in the same way the first farmer, Cain, was born. They still face the same basic problems and challenges that past cultures and civilizations have faced.

Your Bible contains the answers to all your needs in every realm. It matters not whether it be salvation, child-rearing, or basic living. There is a parallel among the problems of the farmer in ancient Israel, the pioneer on the early frontier, and the astronaut in space. The dilemma is not that the Word of God does not contain the answers to the most important questions of life. The problem is that many of us do not have command of enough farm knowledge to understand fully what it says.

God's Principles Do Not Change

Just because we do not fully understand God's laws of the harvest does not mean they are not still in operation. Not one of God's laws is dependent upon your understanding of it for it to work. God's laws operate, not because of your knowledge of them, but *in spite of your knowledge of them.*

Just because I do not fully understand the law of gravity does not mean it will not operate on my body. I won't just float off the planet because I don't happen to know all there is to know about it. If I step off the top floor of the Empire State Building, my ignorance of God's law of gravity will not excuse me from its consequences.

The laws of the harvest operate whether you understand them or not. If you understand and obey them, they will bless you with a harvest. If you are ignorant of them, they will operate against you, leaving you in shortage instead of abundance.

Every Christian who wants to be set free in finances must understand God's financial principles.

When I realized how ignorant I was about basic farming principles, I made up my mind to learn something about them. As I did, I learned God's laws of the financial harvest are the same as His laws of the agricultural harvest.

Let's explore these laws of the harvest:

Law I
Your Seed Must Be Planted

... [There is] a time to plant, and a time to
pluck up that which is planted.
Ecclesiastes 3:2

The writer of Genesis quotes God as saying:

While the earth remaineth, seedtime and
harvest ... shall not cease.
Genesis 8:22

Jesus reinforced this truth in John 12:24 when He said that if a grain of wheat doesn't fall into the ground (seedtime), it abides alone (never multiplies into a harvest).

This is a truth you must understand if you expect to reap the harvest God promises, be it financial or otherwise. Many Christians live their entire lives without ever understanding that *giving is absolutely essential to reaping a harvest.* No matter how fertile the soil, no matter how strong the seed, if the seed does not get planted, it will abide alone. It cannot multiply and become a harvest.

Please understand, unplanted seeds (natural ones) do have their uses. They can be used directly for good nutritious food, for making jewelry, feeding livestock, etc. However, not one seed used in those ways will multiply. It must fall into the earth as a result of your direct effort and will. Your seed must be planted before it can multiply! This is the same for natural seed (wheat, corn, soybeans, etc.) as with other seed — finances, love, loyalty, and possessions.

Many Christians have problems with understanding this simple principle. It does not matter how great your need is. It does not matter how sincere and religious you are. God's laws of the harvest must be followed to reap the harvest.

The most popular New Testament verse dealing with receiving or reaping begins with this simple condition: something first must be given.

> **Give, and it shall be given unto you; good measure, pressed down, and shaken together, and running over, shall men give into your bosom. For with the same measure that ye mete withal it shall be measured to you again.**
> **Luke 6:38**

This same law is also true in the world system. Without making an investment, not one bank or financial institution will give you an increase.

God is far more generous than the bank. He doesn't require minimum deposits or lengthy times of deposit. However, He isn't a fool just because He is generous. God still requires a deposit to be made before an increase can be realized.

> **Be not deceived; God is not mocked: for whatsoever a man soweth, that shall he also reap.**
> **Galatians 6:7**

Your seed must be planted. Allow this first law of the harvest to sink deep into your spirit. Its benefit, along with those of the other laws, will keep you in abundance.

Law II
You Must Render Your Seed Useless

> . . . Except a corn of wheat fall into the
> ground *and die,* it abideth alone. . . .
> **John 12:24**

Christians often give so that their seed gives them
some personal benefit. This is not the way God wants you
to give. King David was once faced with an opportunity to
do this. Because the place of sacrifice was far from his
home, it was necessary for David to buy sacrificial animals
from a local landowner. The landowner very graciously
offered to supply the animals free of charge. David quickly
rejected this gift. He wisely refused to sacrifice to God that
which had cost him nothing.

> . . . Neither will I offer burnt offerings unto
> the Lord my God of that which doth cost me
> nothing. . . .
> **2 Samuel 24:24**

David knew that an offering which cost him nothing
would bring him absolutely no benefits from God.
Throughout the Church, I constantly meet people who
seem to be ignorant of this important principle. They are
giving if it doesn't cost them anything, or only if there is
some secondary benefit to themselves.

> Verily, verily, I say unto you, Except a corn
> of wheat fall into the ground and die, it abideth
> alone: but if it die, it bringeth forth much fruit.
> **John 12:24**

When He said seed must die before it can multiply,
the Lord meant it must enter a stage of uselessness to its

planter. It can't be sold or eaten; it must become totally useless to him.

This same thing must happen to our financial seed when it is sown into the Lord's work. It must leave our control and cease to benefit us. It must be given totally into the hands and control of those who preach the gospel.

Unfortunately, altogether too many Christians do not allow their seed to become useless to them. A common, yet sad example is parents helping children through hard financial times resulting from unemployment, divorce, etc. I often hear these people say they are giving part of their tithes and offerings to help their children. Please don't misunderstand. First Timothy 5:8 tells us to provide for our own. However, listen to this:

> **Bring ye all the tithes into the storehouse,**
> **that there may be meat in mine house. . . .**
> **Malachi 3:10**

It does not say to bring a portion of your tithe to your daughter's house that there may be food in her house. Instead, it clearly says to bring all the tithe into God's house that there may be meat in His house. Using the tithe or offering for our personal needs and obligations does not let the seed die, or multiply.

Give God that which is His and trust Him to supply the extra finances needed to meet additional expenses you face.

Another mistake I find often is that Christians neglect their obligation to tithe and give offerings now, with the rationale that they are designating a large portion of their estate to the Church when they die. They feel sure that

God is pleased, and they have their money to enjoy life with now. However, a person who does this is not giving anything to God. Rather, he or she is leaving it to God. There is a difference. When money is planted regularly, it can bring forth a fruitful harvest, thereby providing more for the giver and for God.

If you desire to reap a financial harvest, you must follow God's laws of the harvest. Your seed must be planted without any secondary benefits to you.

Law III
You Must Plant What You Expect to Harvest

> **. . . the earth brought forth grass, and herb yielding seed after his kind. . . .**
> **Genesis 1:12**

It has been said that the biggest fool is the one who fools himself. Believe it or not, it happens all the time. God warns us of this folly in the matter of sowing and reaping.

> ***Be not deceived;*** **God is not mocked: for whatsoever a man soweth, that shall he also reap.**
> **Galatians 6:7**

This law is set in time and eternity. It is irreversible. The seed you plant determines the kind of harvest you will reap. By some ingenious method, you might disguise an orange seed as a lemon seed and even fool yourself into believing it. However, after the seed is planted and the tree grown, it will bear oranges, not lemons, because you will reap what you sow, oranges.

I cannot stress this point strongly enough. It is not the kind of harvest you need that determines the kind of harvest you will receive. It is the kind of seed you plant that determines the kind of harvest you will reap. Don't fool yourself.

Give, and *it* shall be given unto you . . . .
Luke 6:38

Notice the word *it,* a large and powerful word for having only two letters. Let me paraphrase. Give apples, and *it* (apples) will be given unto you. Give clothing, and *it* (clothing) will be given unto you. Give money, and *it* (money) will be given unto you. You cannot sow clothing and reap retirement income.

Don't fool yourself. If you seek a financial harvest, you must plant money seed.

Law IV
Your Harvest Size Is Established When Your Seed Is Sown

. . . remember this — if you give little, you will get little. A farmer who plants just a few seeds will get only a small crop, but if he plants much, he will reap much.
2 Corinthians 9:6 TLB

No matter how convenient it would be, you cannot wait until the day of the harvest to decide how big a harvest you want. That was determined back when you planted the seed. There is always a season between the time of sowing and the time of harvesting. So you must decide well in advance if you want a bountiful harvest, just an adequate one, or none at all.

I have made an interesting observation during my adult years. It is much easier to adjust to the problem of having more than enough than it is to adjust to the problem of having too little. Wise farmers always plant more than they might need. It is easier to deal with too much rather than too little!

As unbelievable as it sounds, I have heard Christian people say they did not need to give much to God because they did not need much to be happy. By some misguided piety, they reasoned it was spiritual not to desire more than enough. Ignorance of God's purpose brings men to this decidedly unscriptural conclusion.

Dear Christian friend, you cannot be what God is calling you to be if you have only enough. You need more than enough to be a good Christian. With only enough, you are assured of not having enough to do God's will or fulfill the covenant God made with Abraham. Remember, you are the seed of Abraham:

> . . . if ye be Christ's, then are ye Abraham's
> seed, and heirs according to the promise.
> **Galatians 3:29**

What did God promise the world that you, the seed of Abraham would be?

> And I will make of thee a great nation, and I will bless thee, and make thy name great; and thou shalt be a blessing:
> And I will bless them that bless thee, and curse him that curseth thee: *and in thee shall all families of the earth be blessed.*
> **Genesis 12:2,3**

You are meant to be a blessing. How can you be a blessing to anyone, much less all the families of the world, unless you have been blessed? In James 2:15-17, we are told to feed the hungry and clothe the naked. How can you possibly feed and clothe others if you have *only enough* to feed and clothe yourself?

God wants abundance in your life so that you can not only meet all your own needs, but cheerfully bless and meet the needs of others. It is so much easier to be a blessing when you have both planted and harvested much.

Determine what you want to harvest now. Then begin planting the necessary amount of seed.

Law V
Your Seed Must Be Planted in Good Ground

> But other [seed] fell into good ground, and brought forth . . . some an hundredfold, some sixtyfold, some thirtyfold.
> Matthew 13:8

The story of the sower planting his seed in four different kinds of ground is well known. Seed spilled along the wayside and not covered is soon eaten by birds or other animals. Seed sown in stony ground with no depth of soil springs up, but soon withers in the heat. Seed sown among thorns or weeds will quickly be choked out. However, seed sown into good ground brings forth the miracle process of multiplication called the "harvest." In harvest, there may be some hundredfold, sixtyfold, or thirtyfold increase.

Just as this law operates in the agricultural world, so it operates in the world of Christian finances.

How do we identify the best ground in which to plant? I thank God for every good gospel-preaching ministry and every local church that operates today. However, we all know that not all ministries preach and teach the full gospel. By this knowledge, we can conclude that some ground is better than others.

The next four sentences are extremely important; please read them carefully. There are ministries and churches that exist to minister. On the other hand, there are also ministries and churches that minister to exist. One raises money to minister. The other ministers to raise money.

There is an unmistakable characteristic in every good-ground ministry. It will vigorously attempt to accomplish the specific purpose given it by God. How do you recognize good ground? First of all, do not be afraid to investigate, to ask questions, to inspect. A good-ground ministry will not mind answering your questions.

God has also given us an unction.

> . . . ye have an unction from the Holy One,
> and ye know all things.
>
> **1 John 2:20**

With your God-given unction, you can spiritually discern good ground. Discover the good ground and plant in it to reap the harvest God has for you.

Law VI
You Must Always Wait a Period of Time Between Planting and Harvesting

> . . . a man should cast seed into the ground;
> And should sleep, and rise night and day, and the
> seed should spring and grow up . . . .
>
> **Mark 4:26,27**

Faith, as we know, is a key factor in seed planting. A less well known, but equally important factor, is patience. We receive God's blessings through both faith and patience.

> . . . be not slothful, but followers of them who through faith and patience inherit the promises.
> **Hebrews 6:12**

A certain popular scripture is usually quoted this way. "Cast your bread upon the water, and it will come back to you again." While this rendition gives the essence, it leaves out one of the essentials of the verse.

> **Cast thy bread upon the waters: for thou shalt find it** *after many days.*
> **Ecclesiastes 11:1**

It will come back, but only after many days. There is a season between planting and reaping. Faith and patience help us through that season.

> . . . ye have need of patience, that, after ye have done the will of God, ye might receive the promise.
> **Hebrews 10:36**

Lack of patience can cancel your harvest. It can even do that in the realm of worldly finances. If you invest in a Certificate of Deposit (CD) for a specified amount of time, you are guaranteed a return at the end of that time period. However, if you withdraw early, you risk losing a major portion, if not all of the interest you were to reap.

The same is true in the supernatural realm where you have planted your seeds of money. The problem is, it's even easier to cancel your harvest from God. If you allow impatience to weaken your faith to the point you are muttering such things as "God's harvest plan isn't working for me," or "I don't think God is going to come through this time," you have cancelled the harvest.

In the spiritual realm, words are powerful. Words of faith or doubt can change things in your life quickly, if not immediately. I am convinced that Christians have missed some of the greatest financial harvests of all time. They simply spoke them out of existence due to impatience. In essence, they were saying, "I cancel my harvest."

Keep your faith. Be patient. If you are obeying the laws of the harvest, it is on its way.

Law VII
You Must Maintain Your Crops for a Proper Harvest

. . . the thorns sprung up, and choked them.
Matthew 13:7

After a farmer selects his crop, decides on the amount of seed to plant, plants it and watches it sprout, he doesn't just sit back and wait for the harvest. He must still nurture and protect the crop until harvest time.

A Christian's financial harvest-to-be must be similarly maintained. In particular, three areas of crop maintenance must be attended to:

1. You must put God and a godly lifestyle first.

> **. . . seek ye first the kingdom of God, and his righteousness; and all these things shall be added unto you.**
> **Matthew 6:33**

You must allow the Kingdom of God to manifest itself in you. Seeking first the Kingdom of God is the process of actively seeking the rulership of Jesus Christ in your life. Seeking His righteousness is pressing forward toward the goal of becoming like Jesus Christ.

2. The evangelism of the world must be a priority.

> ... I will make of thee a great nation, and I will bless thee, and make thy name great; and thou shalt be a blessing:
> And I will bless them that bless thee, and curse him that curseth thee: and in thee shall all families of the earth be blessed.
> **Genesis 12:2,3**

The power to prosper is explicitly promised to those who desire *to be a blessing* instead of wishing only to be blessed. They will be a blessing through the gospel of Jesus Christ by sharing the gospel and meeting the needs of the hungry, the naked, and the homeless.

3. You must discern deception.

The devil has three methods of attack: he tries to tempt, accuse, or deceive. *None of these ways are more powerful than his ability to deceive.* His deception can be devastating! In the parable of the sower in Matthew 13:22, we see that the deceitfulness of riches can cause men to become unfruitful. When your financial harvest begins, do not allow the devil to deceive you by the increase in your wealth. Do not begin to lavish it solely upon yourself. Remember these words:

> Ye ask, and receive not, because ye ask amiss, that ye may consume it upon your lusts.
> **James 4:3**

Allowing yourself to be deceived by the sudden influx of wealth will turn the harvest process around. You can quickly become unfruitful.

You must maintain a clean, godly life, always moving nearer to God. Give the lion's share of your surplus to the evangelism of the world. Stay alert for Satan's deceptions, even in the smallest parts of your life, about where your bounty came from and where it should really go.

Law VIII
You Must Always Sow *to* Your Harvest Size, Not *From* Your Harvest Size

. . . Isaac sowed in that land [of famine],
and received in the same year an hundredfold. . . .
Genesis 26:12

Something I learned from farmers may come as a big shock to you, just as it was to me. The time when a farmer must make his largest and most costly seed purchase is when he can least afford it. This purchase is necessary when he has suffered a previous crop failure. Money is tight; the urge to conserve is great. Yet the farmer must plant more than ever to make up for the shortage caused by the failed crop.

The farmer must plant more seed in more acres to make up for his shortfall. He needs to plant for his biggest harvest when his funds are the shortest.

Unfortunately, too many Christians don't know this basic law of agriculture. They sow *from* their past harvest. If their harvest was large, they tithe and offer larger offerings. If their harvest was small, they tithe and offer smaller offerings. They continue to sow *from* their harvest, rather than doing it God's way and sowing *to* their harvest.

There is no way to calculate how many of God's children are at the bottom of the financial barrel because they violate this most important law. I am convinced the majority of Christians gauge the size of their offerings by the size of their income, instead of by the size of income they desire in the future.

Every church I ever pastored was full of people who allowed their giving to be influenced by adverse economic circumstances. Rumors of factories closing or other economic crises would immediately cause the weekly offering to go down. The fear of insufficiency overshadowed their faith in God.

We are to give according to our desired future harvest, not from past or present shortage. The very fact that you need a greater financial harvest witnesses to the insufficiency of your past harvests. Your natural tendency will be to give according to your financial shortage. Doing this will not solve your problem; it will only prolong and intensify it.

Faith-promise giving may be the answer for you. Give what you can now, and pay the rest of your promise in regular payments. With faith-promise giving, you are obligated to give only if God supplies you. Remember this, God never fails.

If your past harvests have been sufficient for you and the work God has asked you to do, you are probably planting enough. If your harvests have been less than enough, or if you want to be able to do even more of God's work, you must plant even more than before. When you give more, you will reap more.

Law IX
Your Expense Is Always Highest at Harvest Time

. . . the kingdom of heaven is like unto a man that is an householder, which went out early in the morning to hire laborers into his vineyard.
Matthew 20:1

By now you have learned there are many painstaking steps the farmer must take before he can experience a harvest. He must plant his seed. He must plant in the good ground. He must care for his crops as they grow. As costly as all these steps may be, they are not the most expensive steps he will have to take.

On the day the crop is ripe, the farmer must hire laborers to reap the harvest. Hiring workers incurs his most substantial cost.

In my experience, the same thing is true with financial harvests. While it may not be so readily identifiable as having to hire laborers, there is one additional expense before we can gather our financial harvest. We must expect to give a special, harvest-release offering just as we sense our financial harvest is fully ripe and ready to be reaped.

If you have been sowing regularly and have not yet received your harvest, ask God if this special, harvest-release offering is the key that will bring it forth. Then put this principle to work right now. Write a substantial offering check, and send it to a good-ground ministry to break loose your harvest.

Law X
A Part of Your Harvest Is for Sowing Again

. . . God, who gives seed to the farmer to plant, and later on, good crops to harvest and eat, will give you more and more seed to plant and will make it grow so that you can give away more and more fruit from your harvest.
2 Corinthians 9:10 TLB

A true farmer always saves some seed from each harvest to replant.

Some years ago, I delivered several strong sermons instructing my congregation to put God to the test by planting a substantial financial seed into the ministry. I asked that they report back to me with the results.

I was amazed at how quickly almost everyone received a great financial harvest. The church was astir with testimonies. I was elated. People had learned an important lesson and had received substantial material benefits besides. After a few months, I began questioning people individually to see how they were progressing with subsequent sowing and reaping. I was devastated! I found that only about one out of ten had replanted any seed from their harvest.

The most important part of each and every harvest is not the part you eat, but the part you faithfully plant again. The miracle of the perpetual financial harvest depends on your ability to plant a portion of each harvest back into the gospel.

You can harvest over and over again as long as you plant from each harvest. Yes, you can harvest until Jesus returns if you will not grow weary in well doing, and sow again from each new harvest.

Law XI
A Part of the Harvest Is for You to Keep

> ... who planteth a vineyard, and eateth not
> of the fruit thereof? ...
> **1 Corinthians 9:7**

There are those who teach that Christians are not to have any material possessions, or limited possessions at best. The predominant mentality throughout the Church is that God wants His children to be poor. This idea has left the Church at the edge of bankruptcy, and most church members barely able to survive.

The Bible teaches us of Kingdom stewardship. This is the teaching that God's children are to have all sufficiency to meet all their needs and desires. It doesn't stop there. It goes on to teach that we will have an abundant surplus to give generously into every God-ordained endeavor.

> **God is able to make it up to you by giving
> you everything you need and more, so that there
> will not only be enough for your own needs, but
> plenty left over to give joyfully to others.**
> **2 Corinthians 9:8 TLB**

Throughout the Bible God invites us to eat our fill from the abundance of every harvest He brings forth from our seed. Please do not draw back from enjoying your portion of the harvest because of the misunderstanding of others. If you give in accordance with the laws of the harvest and live a life consistent with God's Word, you will reap a harvest. A substantial portion is for your enjoyment.

Law XII
Your Harvest Is a Miracle

I have planted, Apollos watered; but God gave the increase.
1 Corinthians 3:6

No factory or laboratory has ever manufactured a seed that can reproduce itself into a harvest. Only God can make seed that multiplies. Each and every seed is a miracle capsule that with proper planting and care will reproduce itself.

Always remember that when a harvest occurs, be it agricultural or financial, a miracle has taken place. Harvest always necessitates the intervention of God. There can be no harvest without Him. He is the giver of life.

You must diligently seek after and acknowledge the Lord's participation in every harvest. Without God's intervention, it may be impossible for you to reap a harvest. Seek His help, and command your seed to come forth in Jesus' name. Let your faith be strong.

Therefore I say unto you, What things soever ye desire [your harvest], when ye pray, believe that ye receive them, and ye shall have them.
Mark 11:24

You must shield your faith from doubt. You must speak only words of victory concerning your financial harvest, not defeat. Petition God in prayer for an abundant harvest. Your Heavenly Father will hear. He will act. His miracle, your harvest, will bless you.

Part III

Debt: Its Responsibility,

Its Reduction

5

Debt

Up to Our Eyeballs in Debt!

... the borrower is servant to the lender.
Proverbs 22:7

The amount of money the average family owes to banks, department stores, and other lending institutions has risen every year for the past thirty years. Consumer debt has increased at an even higher rate than the cost of living. It now represents a much larger *percentage* of the average worker's earnings.

Thirty years ago, only about 10 percent of individual earnings was being spent on consumer debt. Today, that figure has risen to a staggering 19 percent. That means almost one-fifth of the average person's earnings is now spent to service his ever-increasing debt!

American consumer debt grew by almost $50 billion in the twelve months of 1988. This amount brought the total to about $700 billion! If this enormous debt were to be evenly divided among every man, woman, and child in the United States, they would each owe about $2,800. Now, mind you, that is only consumer debt. This figure does not include the more than $1 trillion (1,000 billion) that the American public owes to various lending institutions on their home mortgages.

The Wild Card

Today, plastic credit cards make consumer borrowing easier than ever before. These cards are rapidly adding to the whopping debt that now takes 19 percent of all household income.

Credit cards are much easier to abuse than bank loans. The reason is that they do not require the borrower to fill out lengthy forms. Neither do they require him personally to sit down with a loan officer and discuss his ability to repay. Instead, many pre-approved credit cards now arrive through the mail. No consultation with the bank is necessary, so the already over-extended borrower can go out that very day and add $500 to $2,500 to his debt.

Large-scale distribution of pre-approved credit cards is unique to our generation. Before their advent, American Christians were not nearly so predisposed to purchasing consumer goods on credit. Easy access to these plastic charge cards has resulted in the Christian community finding itself in a position of higher debt than ever before. This one strategy of the devil has done more to enslave God's children than any other.

Credit-Card Junkies

Many people in our generation are actually *addicted to credit spending.* These people have been given their own special name. They are called "credit-card junkies." Just like the *junk-food junkies* who cannot control their appetite for unhealthy foods, these financial junkies cannot control their appetite for *compulsive buying.*

This compulsion quickly finds them over their heads in debt. These impulsive spenders do not give a moment's consideration to how their actions will effect their already limited finances. With the mere presentation of their *plastic power,* they can plunge themselves and the ones they love yet further into the bottomless pit of debt.

One recent news story told of a man who owed the unbelievable amount of $67,000 on his multiple credit cards. With this balance, his minimum payment was over $6,200 per month. This amount represented *twice* his entire family's monthly income.

Pre-approved credit cards in the hands of a compulsive shopper can spell the end of that person's happiness. It can cause him to lose *everything he has.*

Plastic Status Symbol

The credit card has become *a status symbol of adulthood.* We all probably know a young person, just fresh out of high school, who proudly displays his first credit card. He now has plastic power to add to his status. Everyone is immediately impressed, especially his admiring parents. He seems so mature, until the card is charged to its limit in the first month.

A bank in Denver, Colorado, has announced a plan to issue credit cards to children as young as *twelve years old!* It is hard to believe a society can be this irresponsible and continue to exist. Surely the writer of Proverbs was correct when he said:

> **Train up a child in the way he should go:**
> **and when he is old, he will not depart from it.**
> **The rich ruleth over the poor, and *the***
> ***borrower is servant to the lender.***
> **Proverbs 22:6,7**

What more can be said? Credit cards are one of the primary contributors to the debt problems of the American family. If it were only the problem of the non-Christian, it would be terrifying enough, but this same mania is rampant in the Church. Plastic power has quickly driven the average Christian to his knees, not in prayer, but under the load of debt he must now bear.

Skyrocketing Bankruptcies

Naturally, with our nation's steadily increasing credit-card debt, comes a steadily decreasing ability to pay that debt. Daily television commercials encourage those with financial difficulty to come on down to the attorney's conveniently located offices, and he will make your money problems just go away. All of this will be done by the world's miracle of debt cancellation: *bankruptcy!*

Since 1984, there has been a sharp increase in personal bankruptcies across our nation. This number reached an alarming 550,000 cases in 1988. Then it went up 90 percent from 1984 to 1990! That's a 90 percent increase in just six years!

The ease of getting into debt with credit cards, and the willingness of consumers to use them, are the major contributors to this skyrocketing increase. Add the recent liberalization of the bankruptcy laws of the federal government, and the removal of the *social stigma* of bankruptcy itself, and you have an *explosive situation.*

The Counterfeit Miracle

Have you noticed there is always a counterfeit to God's miracle? Instant debt cancellation through bankruptcy is no exception. It is an attempt by the devil to counterfeit God's miraculous cancellation of debt, *but do not be deceived.* The world's ways are not God's way.

For my thoughts are not your thoughts,
neither are your ways my ways, saith the Lord.
Isaiah 55:8

Please note, I am not against the bankruptcy laws of our land. They are not wrong when they are applied for their *intended purposes.* There are circumstances in which they are very good. However, they are *immoral* when they become an *easy fix* for irresponsible, reckless spending.

The Banks Own Our Nation's Homes!

The one material thing that Americans have traditionally treasured throughout the decades is *individual home ownership.* Now the very homes that provide the foundation of the American dream, and in most cases, the primary source of financial security, are being placed in *great jeopardy.*

The American tradition has always been for a young couple to purchase a home so that in their senior years, the home is debt free. This plan has operated as a form of security for them in their retirement years, but *not anymore.* Instead, when the mortgage is paid down, the banks are now openly encouraging home owners to borrow against their equity. Here is the shocking truth to this deception. *Thirty percent of all home equity loans are used to repay other debts!*

The federal government has actually helped encourage this type of borrowing, for home mortgage interest is one of the few tax deductions remaining for the average American.

Now the purchase of new cars or other *high-ticket items* is being called a "tax-smart move" when bought through second and third mortgages on the home. This type of purchase is being recommended by financial planners and many tax experts, because the interest can still be deducted. As a result, home equity (retirement security) has little opportunity to build. The participant remains deep in debt for the entire span of his life. He never builds the much-needed, retirement nest egg the debt-free home affords!

Your Hidden Debt

Most people would be shocked if they understood just how great a hold the spirit of debt has on our nation. The average American had to work 124 days in 1989 — a whopping 34 percent of the year — just to pay his federal, state, and local taxes!

Talk about being in bondage to the creditor! You had to work *four full months* of the year just to pay your taxes! (Please keep in mind that this does not include even one of your personal debts.)

In 1989, "Tax Freedom Day," the day the average American finally paid off his tax debt, was May 4. Each year this date is pushed a few days farther into the year.

Looking at it on a daily basis, the average worker toiled two hours and forty-three minutes out of every eight-hour day to satisfy his 1989 tax debt! This means that every day, you had to work two hours and forty-three minutes for the government before you began to earn any money for yourself.

In 1981, the American worker paid Social Security taxes at the rate of 6.65 percent of the first $29,700 earned, or a total maximum tax of $1,975. In 1989, the Social Security tax rate rose to 7.51 percent of the first $48,000, which equals an unbelievable maximum tax payment of $3,605. Social Security taxes alone went up over 82 percent during those eight years! That is more than a 10 percent increase per year!

Your Total Debt Increases Daily

The federal government collected roughly $1.07 trillion in revenue in 1990. That was up $86 billion from 1989. Surely this was enough, but, no! The Congressional Budget Office still predicted a $155 billion deficit!

In March of 1989 alone, the nation's budget deficit reached a staggering $35.78 billion. That's up 22.2 percent from the same month just a year earlier!

Although federal revenues were increased 3.9 percent, government spending shot up 9.5 percent. A year earlier, President Bush's administration estimated the 1989 deficit would total $163.3 billion. That was an increase of 5.3 percent from the $155.1 billion shortfall posted in fiscal 1988.

Here's a number that should stagger your imagination:

$2,775,874,961,565.00

That figure was calculated on April 17, 1989, by the bureau of Public Debt. It represents the total indebtedness of the government of the United States of America on that day. That is how much money we, the American public, owed, and the amount has steadily grown since then.

On average, the national debt grows at the rate of $722 million per day! This means that by August 17, 1989, just four months later, the government's debt had gone up approximately another $87 billion! It shows no sign of stopping. It just keeps getting worse!

You Pay for the Banker's Party

On August 9, 1989, President Bush signed into law the biggest taxpayer bailout in history! The cost for the bailout of the savings and loan industry is staggering. Estimates are that it will total over $1,000 for every man, woman, and child in the United States before it is complete. The estimated cost is $306 billion. That is bigger than the bailouts of Chrysler Corporation, Lockheed, New York City, and the postwar Marshall Plan combined.

To show you just how blind a nation can become, just hear what else took place. In the same month, Congress easily passed a foreign aid package to send $14.3 billion to other nations, including $3 billion for Israel, $2.1 billion for Egypt, and $85 million in military aid to the newly elected government of El Salvador.

Also in that same month, President Bush announced the cancellation of the debt of sub-Saharan African countries to the United States, an amount that is said to be $4.3 billion!

By now, your head is probably dizzy from all these huge numbers, so let me bring it all down to statistics that will make some sense to you. If you had all of your own personal debts paid off, and if you did not owe anybody anything, your personal share of the debt of our federal government would still be *$11,209.54*. Remember, this is the amount each man, woman, boy, and girl owes. If you are the average American family, you have a spouse and two children. That means your total family debt is $44,838.16! (If you have more than two children, add $11,209.54 for each additional child.)

This debt increases about $3 each day for every man, woman, and child. In one year, that amounts to $1,095. This dollar amount represents what the federal government has spent, above the amount they have collected. This is over and above the taxes you have already worked until May 4th to pay!

The World Is Drunk on Debt!

The spirit of debt is not limited to America. Mexico, for example, is currently suffocating under an unmanageable debt load. In 1970, the foreign debt of Mexico was less than $5 billion. In just nineteen years, it grew to $100 billion.

In 1989, Mexico had to pay $7 billion in principal payments and an unbelievable $12 billion in interest to its multitude of creditors. The $19 billion *debt payment* Mexico had for 1989 was almost four times the amount of their *total debt* in 1970! President Carlos Salinas de

Gortari stated, "The foreign debt burden has put the brakes on our national progress. It threatens to break up the entire social and economic fiber of the Mexican community. If this excessive transfer of our resources abroad persists, all will be lost."

Third-world developing countries now owe a total debt of $1.3 trillion. In 1987, sub-Saharan Africa alone owed $137.8 billion in medium- and long-range debt. The amount of the payment to service these debts rose from $5.6 billion in 1979 to $21 billion in 1989. That is a 400 percent increase in ten years, or 40 percent per year.

The spirit of debt is rapidly spreading across the earth. It is more infectious than any other disease on the planet. During the 1980s, Americans, like their government and the governments of other countries, overdosed on deficit spending and debt. This debt has brought us to the 1990s with nothing more than *promissory notes in the coffers of the world.*

Going Under in Good Times

Credit counseling services reported a shocking 67 percent increase in the number of clients coming in for help between 1985 and 1989. This rapid increase of people owing more money than they could repay would be somewhat understandable if our economy had been in a state of depression, but it wasn't! This increase of financial problems took place in the midst of unprecedented financial growth in the American economy!

A Federal Reserve Board economist in Washington, D.C., says historical patterns have gone crazy. It seems contrary to logic that so many Americans would owe so much when financial growth across the nation has been rampant.

Tipping Instead of Tithing

The April 1988 issue of *Christian Retailing* carried an article by Ralph Rath which revealed that the average charismatic Christian spends only $2.17 per week on all Christian-related items. Mind you, that's not just in tithes and offerings. It represents what he spends on *all* Christian causes!

Let this knowledge sink in! American Christians spend 34 percent of their wages to pay Caesar (the government), while they spend less than 2 percent on all Christian endeavors combined. This amount leaves God with nothing more than a tip![1]

A Prophetic Word

Starting right now, the word from God to His Church is, *"Get out of debt!"* The 1990s will be perilous years for planet earth. The creditor is at the world's door, and *the mortgage is due.* There is nowhere to hide. Pastors used to preach about payday someday. Well, that day has come, and the *cupboard is bare.*

The spirit of debt has driven the world into a most uncomfortable position. *Individuals,* as well as *nations,* find themselves up to their eyeballs in debt. They do not seem to realize that the end of the good life is soon to

---

1   *All statistics were compiled by Christian Services Network, El Cajon, California.*

come, even though every day it becomes more obvious that ever-increasing debt cannot continue.

Worst of all, Christians have blindly followed the lost into this pit. Oh, that they might wake up before *the trap closes behind them!*

Is any thing too hard for the Lord? . . .
Genesis 18:14

A strong sense of hopelessness . . . That is the way many Christians describe their inner feelings about their finances. They feel as if they are aimlessly adrift in an endless stream of borrowing. Unpaid bills occupy more and more of their thoughts. They honestly believe there is no way out of their debt dilemma.

Please note that I am not speaking of dishonest people, but hard-working, honest folks who are doing all they know to do. However, try as they may, they keep sliding further and further into debt.

The Joy Is Gone

In most homes, both husband and wife are forced to work. Yet, even with two wage-earners, money always seems to be in scarce supply.

For most families, the joy is gone from payday. All that remains is the Friday night ritual of rushing the paycheck to the bank so that the checks they wrote Thursday will not bounce. After the paycheck is deposited, they draw out a few dollars from the automatic teller machine for their once-a-week, Friday-night splurge. This consists of a modest meal at a fast-food restaurant and a short walk through the mall. Long gone are the days of shopping, for *they must now pay for their past credit sprees.*

For a pitiful, few hours, the wage-earner feels good, enjoying a small portion of the fruit of his labor. All too soon, Saturday morning arrives, and with it comes the full reality of the fruit of debt. The wage-earner must now face his *mountain of bills,* bills that were only partially paid last payday.

God Is Left Holding the Bag

Check after check is written until, finally, the last pressing obligation is paid. With this task accomplished, the stark reality comes to light. There is only enough left to barely scrape by until next payday.

In the crushing pressure of having only enough to make ends meet, *the tithe,* which is vital to receiving God's blessings in life, is usually ignored. At best only a portion of it is paid. This action is usually justified with a promise that soon things will be better, and then God will get what is His.

For the next six days, the average wage-earner has to put off having any fun or doing anything special. To the Christian, the most painful part of his existence is *having to say no to God concerning giving into His Kingdom.* This is an empty cycle that is routinely made from Friday to Friday by those who have come under the control of the spirit of debt.

Wake up! That's no way for the children of God to live. Surely this is not God's best for your life. He must have a better plan.

A Progressive Walk

God is just as concerned about your financial success as He is about every other part of your life.

When you first started to walk with Him, you had to learn to recognize the lies of the devil. They were holding you captive. The world had taught you that drinking and parties were the fun way to live. However, as you progressed in your Christian walk, you realized that kind of thinking is flawed. You began to understand that drinking almost always leads to alcoholism, and wild parties open the door to sexual sins. You found that if you were to experience God's best, you would have to say no to sin, and yes to God's way of doing things.

The further you walked in God's ways, the less complicated your world became. Inner peace began to grow. Much to your own surprise, you started having more fun instead of less fun. Since the troubles and torments that accompany the world's wicked ways had begun to melt away, your life became much more worthwhile.

Well, child of God, I've got good news for you. The same freedom you are experiencing in this area of your life is also available to you with regard to debt!

Recognize the Cause of Your Problem

Before you can participate in this miracle transition, it is important that you recognize some things. *Lies and deceptions* are responsible for your paycheck-to-paycheck existence. Following the world's system of finance instead of God's way is what has brought you to financial shambles. Make no mistake about it. *The world system has enslaved you.*

You must identify the subtle deceptions of this system. You must see how these lies have drawn you into your current financial problems.

The Die Is Cast in Early Childhood

Most Americans bring up their children in homes with *thirty-year mortgages.* They deliver those same precious children to neighborhood schools in the latest, most up-to-date automobiles with *five-year loans.* They buy these children new school clothes with plastic credit cards that charge as high as *21 percent interest* per year! They wash those same clothes in washing machines financed on the *revolving charge account* at the department store.

Their children sleep on *mortgaged beds.* They sit on *mortgaged furniture.* They watch a large-screen, color *television set* which will hopefully be paid off before it falters and breaks down. *Vacations* are routinely paid for with convenient *monthly payments.* The children do their homework using *encyclopedias and computers* bought on *credit.*

The average Christian child is *born into a family that is in debt.* During his childhood, he *never sees that family come out of debt.* Is it any wonder that after eighteen years of development under this influence, the spirit of debt has been transferred to this impressionable child?

The Ritual of Maturity

Debt has become a ritual of maturity in America. Upon graduation from high school, parents proudly take their child down to the local bank. There they lovingly co-sign a loan for his very first car. With this action, they unwittingly launch him into his own *ocean of red ink.*

Parents do this, sincerely believing they have given their child a real head start by establishing his credit rating early!

That's crazy! How much of a head start is this innocent child really receiving? He will probably begin his adulthood earning little more than minimum wage, yet he will owe the bank between five and fifteen thousand dollars on, of all things, a rapidly depreciating automobile!

This new debt has not helped him out one bit. Instead, his parents have just given their permission for the bank to hold their precious child in bondage. They have helped him pledge 1,000 to 3,000 hours of his life to serve the lender!

If what I am saying sounds too harsh, just think about it for a few minutes. Remember, any truth that goes against common beliefs is never accepted easily. Please keep your spirit open, and *consider the entire matter before you react*. I am teaching a *tradition-breaking truth!*

This young adult is now deeply indebted to the bank. He has promised to pay them a whopping *twenty-five to seventy-five weeks of his pay*. This represents six months or more of his meager wages. It is an obligation that can take as much as five years of his life to fulfill. If that's not a form of bondage, *what is it?*

A Basic Premise Is Ignored

Now, what makes this premature initiation into debt even more amazing is that it is done without understanding that a basic scriptural premise is being ignored. When we bring up our children in this kind of debt-laden atmosphere, we overlook one of *God's clear warnings.*

> **Train up a child in the way he should go:**
> **and when he is old, he will not depart from it.**
> **Proverbs 22:6**

Wait, there's more. There is a startling truth that the Church must learn. Scripture taken out of its biblical context usually does not clearly convey the message of God. Instead it conveys the meager thoughts of man. In our everyday interpretation of this verse, the importance of early training is said to be the main lesson. However, if you want some real revelation, look at this often-quoted scripture in its full context.

> **Train up a child in the way he should go:**
> **and when he is old, he will not depart from it.**
> **The rich ruleth over the poor, and the**
> **borrower is servant to the lender.**
> **Proverbs 22:6,7**

Amazing! Train a child to function in debt, and that child will not depart from it when he becomes an adult! How in the debt-ridden world have we overlooked this most obvious scriptural warning? Let that sink into your spirit for a moment; then read verse seven again.

> **The rich ruleth over the poor, and the**
> **borrower is servant to the lender.**
> **Proverbs 22:7**

Do you see what we have been missing? Train up your child to be a debtor, and you have sentenced that child to *a lifetime of servitude to the lender!*

When you consider the clear teaching of these two dynamic verses in their biblical context, you have but one rational choice. *A drastic change* must take place in your thinking and in the thinking of your children. Otherwise, generation after generation will continue to march their unsuspecting children down this deceptive road *into the eager clutches of the spirit of debt.*

A Miracle Is Needed

When I speak of a drastic change, I mean nothing short of a miracle, *a miracle that will rapidly take you out of debt.*

Does such a miracle exist? Can we actually go forward in some financial healing line and walk away with all of our bills marked *paid in full?*

"Why, Brother John, if that were so, the person who had that power should immediately bring this miracle to every family in the world. That's not all he should do! He should then go to every church that is under the bondage of debt, and set them free."

If this type of logic has a familiar ring, it should! It is the same reasoning used by those who are skeptical of miracle healing. Those same sincere folks say, "If anyone really had the power to heal people, he should go to every hospital and heal everyone."

If there were a man alive today who could miraculously heal people, he would be insensitive if he did not at least heal all the sick folks he met. In the same way, if there were a person who could miraculously release people from the awful burden of their debts, that person would be mean indeed if he did not do so.

Before we go any further, let us get one thing straight. No man has the ability to heal anyone miraculously! *Neither is there anyone who can miraculously release people from their debts!* Beloved, the fallacy of this thinking is that miracles are from *men*. They are not from men. Miracles are given by *God* and received, through faith, by men.

I have laid hands on many people and seen them healed; however, *I have never healed anyone.* Each time someone has been miraculously healed, that person had to receive the miracle from God.

The same biblical principle applies to *the miraculous release from debt.* Each time the miracle of debt cancellation takes place, it comes directly from God to those who receive it through faith.

A Widow Received This Miracle

Make no mistake about it. The miracle of cancelled debt is taught in God's Word. One powerful illustration involves a widow woman and her two sons.

This widow was left with an enormous debt at her husband's death. She was hopelessly bound until the miracle of debt cancellation set her free. Her debt was so large that her two sons were sentenced to become servants to the creditor. It took everything she had. She was left with nothing more than a small pot of oil. She was brought to the very door of destitution. In her advanced years, she was cruelly sentenced to the life of a beggar.

Thank God for her faith. Her decision not to seek help from the creditor proved to be the wisest move of her life. In the midst of her desperate problem, *she turned to her man of God.* All the creditor could offer her was *more debt,* but God presented her with the opportunity to receive the miracle of cancelled debt. All she had to do was exercise the faith to do exactly what her man of God told her to do.

The following verses tell us about her powerful miracle of debt cancellation.

> Now there cried a certain woman . . . unto Elisha, saying, Thy servant my husband is dead . . . and *the creditor is come* to take unto him my two sons to be bondmen.
>
> And Elisha said unto her . . . what hast thou in the house? And she said . . . a pot of oil.
>
> Then he said, Go, borrow thee vessels . . .
>
> And when thou art come in, thou shalt . . . pour out into all those vessels, and thou shalt *set aside that which is full.* . . .
>
> And it came to pass, when the vessels were full . . . the oil stayed.
>
> Then she came and told the man of God. And he said, *Go, sell the oil, and pay thy debt* . . . .
>
> **2 Kings 4:1-7**

There it is, right from the pages of your own Bible — a miraculous cancellation of debt! The scriptural account of this particular event opened with an impossible mountain of debt. It demanded payment. Even if it meant the ruination of the woman and her two sons, it had to be paid. Then, in just a few hours, this woman was completely debt free!

With this miracle from God's Word, we see proof positive that He has a miraculous solution for the debt problems of people just like you and me. As you continue to read, you will learn just how badly this miracle is needed!

Debt, a Very Heavy Responsibility!

. . . Alas, master! for it was borrowed.
2 Kings 6:5

The story I'm about to relate to you is true. It comes from the Bible. It is so simple in its truth that most miss its intended meaning. *Debt brings a staggering burden of responsibility upon the borrower.*

We saw how individuals, and even entire countries, suffocate under the burden of debt. Let us now focus on the staggering consequence of debt as it is shown in the Word of God.

The Prophet's Attention Is Captured

The sons of the prophets were in the process of cutting wood for a new dwelling. To obtain the best beams, they went down to the water's edge where the trees grew tall and straight. As one of them was cutting down a tree, the ax head came loose and fell into the water, promptly sinking to the muddy bottom.

At that very moment, the man of God walked by. The young prophet knew he had but a brief moment to draw the prophet's attention to his desperate problem.

You may wonder why the loss of such a simple thing as an ax head would be called a desperate problem. It seems all that was needed was a voucher for the young man to be reimbursed. With the money, he could buy a new ax head, and all would be well.

Before the true depth of this young man's problem can be understood, there is something you must take into account. The Scripture says this was a special ax head, for it was borrowed. When an ax head is borrowed, nothing but the safe return of the same ax head, in the same or better condition, is acceptable.

Fortunately, this young man understood Elisha's heart. He knew the man of God did not want his people to be in debt to anyone. Because of his insight, he did not simply call out, "Sir, I've lost my ax head." Nor did he say that a very good ax head had fallen into the water. He did not cry out to the prophet that the ax head had great sentimental value, or that it had been in the family for years. Any one of these pleas would probably have brought forth no more than a word of sympathy.

Instead, this young fellow guaranteed the involvement of the man of God in retrieving the ax head by crying out that it was *borrowed!*

> . . . and he cried, and said, Alas, master! for it was borrowed.
> **2 Kings 6:5**

Most people do not understand that when they take responsibility for something that is not their own, their entire emotional being will be shaken if it cannot be returned. When the young man realized he could not repay that which he had borrowed, his responsibility for the ax head immediately began to weigh heavily upon him.

Because It Was Borrowed

How did the man of God respond when he heard that the ax head at the bottom of the river had been borrowed? He immediately realized that this matter went far beyond the mere loss of an ax head. Something had to be done.

Everything else had to wait, for the young prophet had allowed himself to become the servant of man (the lender).

> ... the borrower is servant to the lender.
> **Proverbs 22:7**

Nothing short of a miracle could have solved this problem. The young prophet's moment of reckoning was fast approaching. The ax head would soon have to be returned. If it could not be, the testimony of that young man would be tarnished in the eyes of the lender.

Hear the sacred Word as it reveals the prophet's attitude toward the young man's problem.

> **And the man of God said, Where fell it? And he shewed him the place. And he cut down a stick, and cast it in thither; and the iron did swim.**
> **Therefore said he, Take it up to thee. And he put out his hand, and took it.**
> **2 Kings 6:6,7**

One of the most extraordinary miracles ever performed took place. There was no other reason important enough to merit a *swimming ax head* than the fact that it was borrowed. This fact immediately changed the significance of this occasion from a *minor* event to a *major* event.

Often this passage is used to illustrate the power of God. Why, He can even make an iron ax head swim! Beloved, that is not the main point made here. The most important lesson is that *God is concerned about your debt problems!*

Debt Brings Anxiety

Experts tell us that today, as never before, our society is overwhelmed with anxiety. The greatest single reason for this emotional upheaval is attributable to *money problems.* The staggering debt with which most people are forced to live is more than their emotional systems were created to bear.

Please note that I am not speaking of financial deadbeats (those who borrow with no intention of repaying). I am speaking of good, honest people who have foolishly acquired more debt than they can repay. Our society is full of these folks. They suffer tremendous psychological pain. Their inability to manage their debts gives them a feeling of hopelessness.

More sleepless nights are attributed to unmanageable debt than to anything else. This debt has been largely responsible for America's becoming an around-the-clock society. Stores, television stations, and bars remain open twenty-four hours a day, primarily catering to the needs of the sleepless.

A Damaged Fender Can Damage Your Soul

Let me illustrate how devastating the responsibility of debt can be. Have you ever had a little fender-bender with your automobile? When this happens it is traumatic, to say the least. No matter how unpleasant it may be, it is not to be compared to the trauma the same fender-bender would cause if the circumstances were just a little different. Imagine that you had this same accident in *a borrowed car.* Upon impact, your inner man (soul) would immediately cry out, *"Alas, it was borrowed!"*

No matter how you try, it is next to impossible to completely remedy the damage done to something borrowed. It will never be the same again. You can even go out and buy a more expensive model to replace it, but from deep down in your soul, the accuser will tell you of your *irresponsibility*. Even if the lender totally forgives you, your soul may be permanently scarred. The impact of not being able to return that which you borrowed in its original condition will leave its mark. Each time you see the one who loaned you the car, you will feel the pain. Personally, I would rather have my own automobile totally destroyed than to put even a scratch on a borrowed car!

When responsible people borrow, their emotions are always impacted. There is no better way to put it. *Borrowing grinds at your insides.*

Debt Attributes to Divorce

Many Christians have a hard time believing God is concerned about their finances. Yet all Christians would agree that God has extreme concern for the sanctity of marriage. Well, beloved, here's a simple fact. Unmanageable debt is the leading cause of broken marriages! In 1988 over 50 percent of the 1.3 million newly divorced couples listed money (or more precisely, more debt than there was money to repay) as *the main reason* for their divorces.

It's no wonder that financial trouble is the leading cause of divorce. When debt is out of control, wives become *afraid* to answer the telephone. They fear hearing the harsh voice of another bill collector demanding payment. They are *afraid* to answer the door because they may be greeted by one of the utility companies that has come to shut off their service. Every time a truck pulls up on their street, they *fear* it is the man from the finance company coming to take back the television or the family car.

With a day of *debt-induced terror* behind her, you can easily imagine the *warm greeting* this housewife is going to give her already stressed-out husband when he walks in the door. Can you imagine the inadequate feelings this husband experiences as he listens to his wife's broken-hearted description of her day? Do you see how debt tears at marriage?

Christian marriages are not exempt! Husbands become threatened, even intimidated, when they fail to provide the basic necessities for their families. This lack strikes at the very essence of the husband's manhood.

Breadwinners Become Bread Losers

Even though many wives work outside the home, the husband is traditionally looked upon as the family's *breadwinner*. However, if he fails to provide bread for the family adequately, at least in his own mind, he becomes the family's *bread loser*. Financial failure causes him embarrassment, making him feel unattractive, even unworthy of his wife's attention. When the husband begins to feel inadequate in providing the basic necessities for his family, that family is well on its way to destruction.

The results are predictable. The most intimate relationships in that marriage start to fall apart. All meaningful communication stops as the relentless *pressure of unpaid bills* increases. Loving care is quickly replaced by *short tempers*. Family fights start over such things as whether or not it is *really* necessary to take junior to the doctor. The real issue ceases to be if the child needs medical attention, but the underlying issue is, *How in the world will we be able to pay another doctor bill?*

Divided Families

This same tragic pattern often repeats itself among other family members. When son borrows from father, or when sister borrows from brother, and fails to pay back the debt, something much more serious than the loss of money takes place. Fathers and sons stop talking. Brothers and sisters cease to visit each other. In short, borrowing from relatives often results in a permanent breach in normal family relations.

Broken Friendships

Bad debts quickly break up *lifelong friendships.* When you borrow money from a friend, then cannot pay it back, what happens? Invariably, the friendship begins to weaken, then it just dies. If the amount of the debt was high enough, lifetime friends are turned into *lifetime enemies.*

Good Employees Become Bad Employees

Alcoholism and drug abuse are often triggered by the pressures of unmanageable debt. Previously good employees are driven to poor work habits, crime, or even suicide over their debt problems. Sleepless nights and meaningless days are the result of not being able to pay the bills. Eventually, a good employee becomes a bad one. Letters of commendation turn into *warning notices,* and eventually, the dreaded *pink slip appears.*

The Great Commission Becomes the Great Omission

The over-extended Christian can have little if any part in the gospel outreach. Instead of his primary purpose being to reach the world for Christ, he must now allocate all his money to debt payments. To put it simply, *his debt now rules him.* He can no longer properly give to the cause of Christ. His new master will not let him. Debt always says no to the preaching of the gospel. For all intents and purposes, the overburdened child of God has, by his own hand, cancelled his part in the great commission.

When the spirit of debt rules, the biggest goal the local church has is making the monthly mortgage payment. Satisfying the lender has replaced satisfying God. When this happens, the church is no longer the servant of God. Her own foolish actions have made her the servant of the lender.

Child of God, I hope the seriousness of this nightmare is beginning to sink into your spirit. *Debt rules! Debt ruins!*

Remember, the Word of God says:

> . . . the borrower is servant to the lender.
> Proverbs 22:7

Forced Bankruptcy Awaits

When you come into uncontrollable debt, no financial decision can be made without first consulting your new ruler, the lender. You cannot go on vacation. You cannot buy desperately needed groceries for the hungry. You cannot even give to the gospel.

Even if the Spirit of God moves you, the lender has the right to say, *"No, I must be paid first!* Until I am paid in full, you are *my* servant, not the Lord's."

When debt rules, it can even decide that your tithe will not be paid! The courts of the land say so. There is a little-known law in the federal bankruptcy statutes that outlines a simple procedure that can be used by anyone to whom you owe money. This provision of the law allows the lender to tell you how you must spend your money.

If any of your creditors feel they are not being fairly paid out of your income, they can have the bankruptcy court intervene in your financial matters. The court can then tell you whom you can and cannot pay. This procedure is called "involuntary bankruptcy," or "creditor-induced bankruptcy." When this is used, the government (Caesar), not God, rules over your finances. You will not be allowed to pay any tithe or offering until every cent is paid to the lenders!

The children of God must understand that when something has been borrowed, the fatal day of reckoning always comes. When it does, nothing short of *payment in full* will satisfy the lender. God knew precisely what He was saying when He declared:

> . . . the borrower is servant to the lender.
> **Proverbs 22:7**

Debt is an extremely severe form of servitude! It is no wonder that a loving God cares so much about people who are in debt—*people like you!* He does not want His children burdened with this heavy responsibility.

If you still cannot believe that God really cares about such basic things as the bills you owe, here is a comforting statement for you.

> Casting *all* your care upon him; for *he careth for you.*
>
> **1 Peter 5:7**

God wants to take the excessive responsibility of debt off your back, "for He careth for you!"

Jesus Had a Debt Miraculously Cancelled

> ... thou shalt find a piece of money. ...
> **Matthew 17:27**

Jesus owed a debt? I beg your pardon! Jesus would never be in debt!

Isn't it strange that we cannot think of our Lord and Savior being in debt? Why, that is not the proper lifestyle for the Son of God! Now, hear me as I speak to your spirit. Whatever lifestyle is not proper for our Lord is not proper for His children either. Scripture is clear on this.

> ... as he is, so are we in this world.
> **1 John 4:17**

> ... we all ... are changed into the same image from glory to glory. ...
> **2 Corinthians 3:18**

Some Debts Are Unavoidable

Debts are incurred by everyone. Sometimes they are not the result of poor financial practices. I know Jesus conducted His business matters in a proper way. The debt

He owed was one everyone will owe. It was in the form of a tax bill.

Now, I call this a "debt" because taxes are always paid in arrears. They are never paid in advance. My wife and I are debt free, so to speak, but we have a bill that never gets paid off. It is our taxes.

Let's read what the Bible says about our Lord's miracle of cancelled debt.

> **And when they were come to Capernaum, they that received tribute money came to Peter, and said, Doth not your master pay tribute?**
> **Matthew 17:24**

The word translated *tribute* is the Greek word that literally means "the double drachma." This was the name of the coin used to pay the temple tax. Yes, Jesus and Peter were faced with a tax bill. Notice that Simon Peter immediately told the tax collector that His master most certainly did pay taxes.

> **He saith, Yes . . . .**
> **Matthew 17:25**

Surely Jesus paid taxes, for He fulfilled all righteousness. Later, Peter himself wrote that we, as Christians, should obey the laws of the land.

> **Submit yourselves to every ordinance of man for the Lord's sake: whether it be to the king, as supreme;**
> **Or unto governors. . . .**
> **1 Peter 2:13,14**

Jesus said to give to the government that which belongs to the government.

> . . . **Render to Caesar the things that are**
> **Caesar's. . . .**
>
> **Mark 12:17**

Jesus Chose the Miraculous

As you look closely, you will see that Jesus actually stopped Simon Peter from paying the debt in the normal way. I believe Peter was on his way into the house to get the tax money from the treasurer, Judas. With this money, he was going to pay the tax bill for Jesus and himself.

> . . . **And when he was come into the house,**
> *Jesus prevented him.* . . .
>
> **Matthew 17:25**

The verse tells us that Jesus stopped him from his planned action, for He had a better plan. This time the debt would not be paid from the treasury. There would be a miraculous cancellation of debt.

Jesus acknowledged the unfair way in which the taxes of this world were being taken.

> . . . **What thinkest thou, Simon? of whom do**
> **the kings of the earth take custom or tribute? of**
> **their own children, or of strangers?**
>
> **Matthew 17:25**

Jesus asked Peter a question that dealt with how the corrupt tax system of this world operated. He asked him if he thought the kings' children had to pay this tax. Simon said, "No, Lord. The strangers have to pay the tax." Jesus was showing Peter that the system controlling the world is corrupt. They tax strangers, and do not tax their own. Jesus quickly told Simon not to get hung up on this inequity. To keep from offending anyone and causing themselves unnecessary trouble, they would pay the tax, *but not out of the treasury.* Instead they would cancel the tax bill with a miracle.

> **Notwithstanding, lest we should offend them, go thou to the sea, and cast an hook, and take up the fish that first cometh up; and when thou hast opened his mouth, thou shalt find a piece of money: that take, and give unto them for me and thee.**
>
> **Matthew 17:27**

When this event is looked at as a miraculous cancellation of debt, it makes most Christians very uncomfortable. We can easily believe the miracle of the coin found in the fish's mouth. However, we do not like the thought that this was a debt cancellation. We especially do not like to hear that this miracle is available to Christians *today.*

He Is Always the Same

We can tolerate a God who cancelled debt in the Old Testament. Why, we are even able to accept that God would cancel debt in the millennium or at His second coming, but a debt-cancelling God *for today* is more than most can believe!

Once again I must say He is:

> **. . . the same yesterday, and to day, and for ever.**
>
> **Hebrews 13:8**

If Jesus performed the miracle of cancelled debt in the past, He will perform it in the present. Peter did nothing to *earn* the payment of that debt. Jesus did nothing to *earn* His tax money either. Both Jesus and Simon Peter were recipients of the miracle of cancelled debt. By a supernatural miracle, Peter pulled a coin from the mouth of a fish. That coin was of sufficient value to pay the tax bill for both of them *in full.*

Never once did Jesus say, "Now, Peter, this is a once-in-a-lifetime miracle, so don't expect it ever to happen again."

Trust in the Man of God Was Needed

One other major point should be considered here. It is of utmost importance to your miracle of cancelled debt. Although Jesus Christ was God Himself, at this time Peter knew Him as only a man. Before the miracle could be manifested, Peter had to be willing to *believe and obey his man of God,* Jesus.

Peter could have said, "Lord, you have got to be kidding. I'm not going to go down to the sea and make a complete fool of myself by looking for money in a fish's mouth. Why, Lord, I am a fisherman. I've looked in fishes' mouths countless times. I have lots of experience with fish, and I have never found a coin in one before!"

If Peter had not believed his man of God, the miraculous cancellation of the tax bill would never have taken place. Peter had a clear-cut choice. *Believe the man of God and prosper, or doubt the man of God and block the prosperity of God.*

> **. . . believe his prophets, so shall ye prosper.**
> **2 Chronicles 20:20**

He chose to believe his man of God, and he prospered. The miracle of cancelled debt was his. Don't you know Peter was glad he trusted his man of God when he saw his tax bill marked *paid in full?*

Getting You Through, Not Out

**All scripture is given by inspiration of God,
and is profitable. . . .**
2 Timothy 3:16

The Scripture is most surely profitable. It has been of benefit to men and women for as long as it has existed. Again and again the Bible has brought salvation, health, and guidance. However, the benefit of the Word of God goes beyond these. It is effective for *every need and want of mankind.*

One of the greatest needs the Church faces today is release from its back-breaking load of debt. By the Church, I mean the individual members as well as the corporate structure. Debt is rampant in our midst.

The Church is hearing more prophecy than it has ever heard about the approaching end of the age. Personally, I have been hearing this message for over thirty years. I am convinced that the second coming of Christ is closer than it has ever been. However, it is evident that this event has not yet taken place.

This fact has caused me to begin to emphasize God's ability *to get us through* the everyday problems of life. For this reason, I have dedicated my ministry to prophesying *the solutions* God has for His people in these last days.

Please do not misquote me! I believe Jesus has the *ability* to return *at any moment.* Personally, I hope He does come soon. However, if He chooses to tarry His coming, I want the children of God to know that the answer to

Satan's end-time strategy of debt is *God's miracle of debt cancellation!*

Today Is Not the Day of Miracles

Now I can just hear someone saying, "Why, Brother John, don't you know we live in New Testament times? God would never perform a miracle of debt cancellation in these days. Haven't you been told *this is not the day of miracles?"*

I must agree. I do not believe in the day of miracles either. However, I do believe in the *God of miracles,* and there have always been people who believe He is able to perform miracles in *the time of their need.* Miracles do not depend upon a *day* for their manifestation. They depend upon the *ability of God,* who performs them.

However, even those who willingly accept the fact that God still performs miracles often resist the possibility that He will still perform the miracle of debt cancellation.

It Serves Them Right

Many Christians feel that those who are in hopeless debt situations deserve the misery they have brought upon themselves. Deliverance for irresponsibility somehow seems wrong. Why, miraculous debt cancellation would be nothing more than letting the spend-thrifts have their cake and eat it too! Those who have carefully budgeted their money just don't think it is fair for those who have purchased every *impulse* item they desire, to get off *scot-free.* They, of all people, *justly deserve* the hard times their reckless spending has brought upon them. Surely they should not be let off the hook with a miracle!

The Elder Brother Spirit

This is the same spirit that overcame the elder brother of the Prodigal Son. He was not disturbed because his brother had squandered all his inheritance. He was angry because his wayward brother did not have to suffer long and hard for his indiscretions.

Please let me warn you. You must guard your heart against this kind of thinking. The spirit of jealousy that results from this attitude *is no better than the spirit of debt it condemns!* Remember, the deliverance of God is *always unmerited.*

No One Is Cheated When God Delivers

When a person is healed of cancer, you never hear anyone complaining, "Well, that miracle just isn't right. The doctors got cheated out of their surgical bills." You don't hear anyone saying the hospital was cheated out of their medical charges. No one says an injustice was done to the mortuary because the healing kept them from getting their fee. No one will claim that others with cancer were cheated because they were not healed.

Well, I know this thinking must sound pretty ridiculous, but I suspect these are the types of thoughts that keep most Christians from rushing to God for debt relief. Inwardly, they believe they deserve the devastation their debt has brought with it.

God Does Not Want to Give You What You Deserve

Think of it! Every lost person deserves to go to hell. Everyone has sinned and come short of the glory of God.

Many people are sick because they have abused their bodies. Those who have smoked two packs of cigarettes a day have surely earned their emphysema. The vast majority of those who are in prison deserve their sentences. However, God is daily working miracles for these same, undeserving people. I never hear anyone say, "Oh, that person deserved cancer!" or "That person deserves to go to hell!"

No one *earns* salvation. No one *earns* healing. No one *earns* God's love. All God's gifts are freely given to those who have faith to receive them. In just this way, the miracle of cancelled debt is freely given. *God wants to perform it because He loves you!*

It Is Not a Religious-Sounding Miracle

We seem to eagerly accept the miracle of salvation in the lives of the grossest sinners. We openly rejoice when those who have abused their health are miraculously healed.

Then, no matter what the circumstances are that bring someone into the clutches of debt, why not accept a miracle of debt cancellation?

When we see a man pictured in an evangelistic magazine with his crutches lifted up toward heaven, we say to ourselves, "Isn't Jesus wonderful? Surely this proves that God still works miracles. He is a good God, for *He is the same yesterday, today, and forever.*"

When we see the flowing tears of a small child who was once blind and can now see, we quickly say, "Isn't Jesus wonderful? He still works miracles. He is a good God, for *He is the same yesterday, today, and forever.*"

You see, healing is a miracle we can easily identify with God. However, much of the Church does not want to hear what the Bible says about money because they think God's financial miracles sound *carnal.*

Child of God, please let it settle into your spirit once and for all. Our God does *more* than open blind eyes. He does *more* than make crippled limbs straight. He does *more* than renew the rotting flesh of the leper. *He also cancels the debts of His people!*

Please add the fact that God can cancel debt to your list of miracles, for *He is the same yesterday, today, and forever!* He has saved before, He has healed before, and He has delivered from the power of debt before.

If you have a debt today, your God can perform a debt-release miracle today. Whatever He did for those in the past, He can do for you in the present. Miracles are available *any day that a child of God has the faith to believe for them.*

More Qualified

I must point out another special truth. Today, you are actually more qualified to receive the miracle of cancelled debt than anyone mentioned in Scripture. The Word of God clearly makes this promise.

After the writer of Hebrews carefully stated the miraculous way in which God moved in the lives of the Old Testament saints, he boldly promised that *something much better is available for us.*

> **God having provided some better thing for us. . . .**
>
> **Hebrews 11:40**

As marvelous as any miracle in the Bible may seem, you have *a scriptural promise of an even better miracle!*

Now, please keep this in mind. The miracle of debt release will not happen because I say it will. It will happen because *the Holy Bible, the perfect Word of God, says it will.*

... let God be true, but every man a liar. ...
Romans 3:4

Your miracle of cancelled debt can be better because you are in a *better relationship with God through a better covenant.*

Remember, miracles are not given out by man. They are always *given by God.* They are almost never given to those who doubt that they can have them. They are given to those who *receive them through unwavering faith.*

... let him ask in faith, nothing wavering. ...
James 1:6

This thought can be taken one step further. Just because a desired miracle does not manifest itself immediately, that does not mean it is not available. When healing does not immediately manifest itself, you do not stop believing that the miracle of healing exists.

The same is true for the miracle of debt cancellation. After you have prayed for it, just continue to do everything in your power to pay off your debt. Keep believing and keep praying. The miracle will take place.

Through the power of faith and patience, God *can and does* intervene in our lives to heal miraculously. In that same way, through the power of faith and patience, He will also miraculously intervene to help you pay your debts.

> . . . be . . . followers of them who through
> faith and patience inherit the promises.
> **Hebrews 6:12**

No circumstance is too difficult for God. He can save; He can heal; He can also break *the death grip of debt* off your life!

You Have Already Manifested Your Greatest Faith

Whenever faith is mentioned, most Christians immediately think of some difficult, mystical task they must perform to get God moving. Let me set your mind at ease. If you are saved, *you have already manifested enough faith* to receive the greatest miracle possible — *the miracle of salvation.*

Yes, when you received your salvation by faith, you received the greatest miracle God has to offer. No miracle can ever be better than the miracle of new life in Jesus Christ.

Now, I must point out that some strange process takes place in most Christians soon after they accept Jesus as their Savior. With the passing of time, they grow weaker in faith instead of stronger. They begin to struggle with the miracle of healing. They struggle with the miracle of restoration of family relationships. They struggle with the miracle of increase in their finances.

For a long time I was puzzled at this strange phenomenon. Then I realized that *unbelief and traditions* work in direct opposition to the Christian's ability to receive.

How Unbelief Begins

Please wake up to this biblical truth. *Unbelief will restrict the miracle-working power of God in your life.*

And he did not many mighty works there because of their unbelief.
Matthew 13:58

I am convinced that unbelief begins with *amazement.* When we are amazed by the miracle power of God as He moves among men, we are damaging our faith. Each time we allow amazement to manifest itself, unbelief is given an open door to enter into our spirits.

When God moves in great power, our reaction should be the exact opposite of amazement. We should actually be amazed only when He does not move. We should be amazed when a broken home we have faithfully prayed for is *not restored!* We should be amazed when the financial needs of a dedicated Christian family are *not met!*

Think about it. *Unbelief finds its roots in amazement!*

When you were a child, you were amazed by the huge airplanes your father took you to see at the airport. It seemed to you as if an impossible event had taken place when they ascended into the heavens like mighty, iron birds. Now that you are older and understand the nature of God's physical laws, the flight of an airplane *no longer leaves you in amazement.* You simply get on board, and *expect* the airplane to rise into the air because you know it can. The truth of the matter is that the whole nation actually gasps in amazement when an airplane *crashes,* not when it takes off.

Amazement comes from not understanding the nature of a thing. For instance, if you knew the professional techniques a magician used to create the illusion of sawing someone in half, your amazement at the trick would immediately cease.

Your amazement at God's movements comes from a lack of understanding of His true nature. When you fully understand God's nature, you will no longer stand amazed at His mighty miracles. You will understand they are part of His normal activity.

Now, do not misunderstand what I have said to you. We should always remain in reverence, even in wonder, of God's sacred miracles, *but not in amazement!* God can do anything the Bible says He can. Behold the wonder of His power! Thank Him for His miraculous intervention in your life! Do not be amazed, for unbelief finds its roots in amazement. It has no place in the mind of the child of God who knows his Lord's abilities.

Is any thing too hard for the Lord? . . .
Genesis 18:14

This verse asks a question that always brings a thunderous no! Yet, we still tend to be amazed when we hear that God has dissolved a cancer, stopped an addiction, or changed the heart of a wayward child.

All of these miracles are easy for God to perform. Our Bible tells us He will do even *greater things* than those recorded in His Word.

Now unto him that is able to do exceeding
abundantly above all that we ask or think,
according to the power that worketh in us.
Ephesians 3:20

The power that works in us to receive miracles is not amazement, but *faith.* God can do anything!

When you fully understand God's divine nature, your *amazement will change to expectation,* for God's nature is unchanging.

> **Jesus Christ the same yesterday, and to day, and for ever.**
>
> **Hebrews 13:8**

When your amazement turns to expectation, *it has turned to faith.* Faith is what expectation is made of.

> **Now faith is the substance [raw material] of things hoped for [expected], the evidence of things not seen.**
>
> **Hebrews 11:1**

How Traditions Weaken Your Faith

How very powerful the Word of God is! It has turned the course of history many times. It has guided conquerors. It has doomed infidels. Its power is *almost* without earthly parallel. Notice I said *almost,* for no matter how powerful the Word of God is, there is a power on planet earth that will render its promises invalid to you. *It is the power of any tradition you hold that is contrary to the Word of God.*

> **. . . Thus have ye made the commandment of God of none effect by your tradition.**
>
> **Matthew 15:6**

Traditions have an unfair advantage over Christians, for they come to us disguised as truth. The very people who loved us enough to bring us to Christ are usually the ones who introduce us to the traditions we receive and defend. No matter how sacred these teachings are, if they don't find their basis in the true interpretation of God's Word, *they must be forsaken.* You cannot move into God's best until you reject religion's best, your traditions.

God Is Stirring a Miracle for You

I feel a miracle beginning to stir in the spirit world for you. Your traditional lifestyle of debt, with its bondage to banks, department stores, and financial institutions, has *made a slave out of you!* This day, *the tradition of being in debt begins to crumble.* God's truth about debt is beginning to flood your spirit. You now know what debt has done to you. It has made you into a servant.

. . . the borrower is servant to the lender.
Proverbs 22:7

Oh, I have wonderful news for you! The miracle that will break the spirit of debt is on its way. In short order this miracle will bring you to the end of the domination of debt. You are about to be set free. The revelation you are receiving from God's Word is leading you out of bondage.

Do not give way to fear. Breaking the power of debt in your life will not be too difficult for you to accomplish. You will be able to take hold of it *by your faith.* Now it will be possible for the Holy Spirit of God to lead you step by step into total debt relief.

Just promise yourself that you will not allow your *traditions* to make the Word of God of no effect. Promise yourself that you will not allow *unbelief* to weaken your faith. If you will help in this way, it will be much easier for God to release you into your new debt-free lifestyle.

Say the following sentence out loud right now. *"I am debt free through the miracle power of God!"*

Say it several more times. Say it until it ceases to amaze you when you hear it. By doing this, you are kicking the bad seeds of tradition and unbelief out of your spirit. You are replacing them with the good seed of God's Word.

Remember, God's miracle of canceled debt is the property of those who are able to believe Him for it.

Keep your *faith* focused on the *God of miracles,* and you will see that He can also perform the miracle of debt cancellation for you!

The Power of Debt Can Be Broken

> . . . devils are subject unto us through thy name.
>
> **Luke 10:17**

Debt is a spirit, and all spirits *must leave* when they are commanded to do so in the *mighty name of Jesus!*

> Behold, I give unto you power to tread on serpents and scorpions, and over *all the power of the enemy.* . . .
>
> **Luke 10:19**

> And whatsoever ye shall ask in my name, that will I do, that the Father may be glorified in the Son.
>
> **John 14:13**

First, Bind the Chief Spirit

God has given us *power* in the spirit world. However, before any problem that arises from demon spirits can be solved, *the chief spirit* must be dealt with.

> . . . how can one enter into a strong man's house, and spoil his goods, except he *first bind the strong man?* and then he will spoil his house.
> **Matthew 12:29**

Debt cancellation must be preceded by *putting a stop to the increase of debt.* The spirit of debt must first be bound from your finances before any significant changes can be accomplished. You will find that behavior modification becomes relatively easy when the chief spirit that caused the adverse behavior is removed.

Twelve Hundred Miles From My Bills

One night a few years ago I was in a telethon in Greenville, North Carolina. God had been showing me from Scripture that there is a spirit of debt. He showed me that not only had this spirit influenced the lost, but it had also driven *most of the Christian world* into the debt lifestyle.

When I departed for the station that night, I knew that before the audience would be able to receive the full prosperity of God, the power of the spirit of debt would have to be broken off their finances. I asked the viewers to gather up their bills and bring them before their television screens. God had told me the people should have their bills in hand when I prayed. This was the first time I had ever rebuked the spirit of debt.

Just before I began to pray, my wife said we also needed this release. At that moment, our own bills were almost twelve hundred miles away. How could we partake under these circumstances?

Immediately the Holy Spirit showed me a way to take the anointing of that moment back home with me to our debts. I told my wife, "Take an offering envelope, and let's hold it up in the place of our bills."

I earnestly prayed, in the name of Jesus, that we and the viewers who joined their faith with ours would receive a release from the spirit of debt. Then my wife and I took that special offering envelope home with us and placed it in the midst of our bills.

Each time one of our bills was paid off, we waived the anointed envelope in the air and proclaimed that the spirit of debt had been forever broken off our lives. We also declared openly that the miracle of cancelled debt had been released to us. Then we placed the anointed envelope back among our bills, speaking only that all the bills would soon be paid in full.

We continued this process for the next few years. Then one day we burned our last bill. It was the mortgage on our parsonage! This was the first time in our thirty years of marriage that my wife and I were totally debt free.

Steps That Will Take You Out of Debt

From my own experience, I can now say that breaking the power of debt will not be nearly so hard for you as the devil would have you believe. However, several definite steps must be taken for you to succeed. Please prayerfully read the following list.

1. You must sit down with a pencil and paper and list every bill you owe. This accounting must be done before you can launch a proper plan of attack against the havoc the spirit of debt has wrought in your personal finances.

This is not a secular approach to your problem. It is prescribed by our Lord Himself.

> **For which of you, intending to build a tower,
> sitteth not down first, and counteth the cost,
> whether he have sufficient to finish it?**
> **Luke 14:28**

Count the cost the spirit of debt has brought to your life. Recognize that it has been the motivating force behind your bills.

When you have the whole picture clearly outlined before you, ask God for the specific financial miracles you need to free you from the bondage of your debt. Remember to be thankful for any progress you make in debt reduction. Your first financial miracle may be *very small,* but acknowledge that it has come from God. Be sure to let principalities and powers know it is not your last financial miracle. There will be many more.

> **. . . faith is the substance of things hoped
> for. . . .**
> **Hebrews 11:1**

If you are not acknowledging financial miracles, they will cease.

2. If at all possible, you should have a relationship with a good local church.

Why is this important? Giving your tithes into good ground is necessary to keep the windows of heaven open over your finances.

> **Bring ye all the tithes into the storehouse,**
> **that there may be meat in mine house, and prove**
> **me now herewith, saith the Lord of hosts, if I will**
> **not open you the windows of heaven. . . .**
> **Malachi 3:10**

You cannot expect to reap financial miracles unless the windows of heaven are open over your life.

3. It is also necessary to associate yourself with some good-ground ministries such as a Christian television station, a Bible teacher, an evangelist, or a missionary.

This relationship is necessary because you will need a good place to give your offerings. Your offerings will provide God with the measure He needs to pour out your financial blessings.

4. The strong man must be bound.

> **. . . how can one enter into a strong man's**
> **house, and spoil his goods, except he *first bind the***
> ***strong man?* . . .**
> **Matthew 12:29**

You must speak specifically to the strong man (the spirit of debt). Tell him he is bound from any further influence in your finances. To put it plainly, he must release his hold on your money. Bind him and cast him from your life. Be sure you do this in the mighty name of Jesus. Remember, His name is infinitely stronger than the spirit of debt. The Bible says:

> **That at the name of Jesus *every* knee should**
> **bow, of things in heaven, and things in earth, and**
> **things under the earth.**
> **Philippians 2:10**

You are not to be afraid when you speak to the spirit of debt. *It is the spirit of debt that must be afraid.* You have something going for you that is bigger and stronger than anything the devil has going for him.

> *. . . greater* **is** *he* **that is** *in you,* **than** *he* **that is**
> *in the world.*
> **1 John 4:4**

(I will lead you in speaking to the spirit of debt in the confession in the next step.)

5. Now lift your bills up before the Lord, and repeat this prayer. Say it out loud.

Dear Lord,

I know you care for me, spirit, soul, and body. Lord, I have many bills. They are a hindrance to me. They keep me from giving to you the way I really want to.

Lord, I believe that Brother John is a true man of God. I believe what he has taught me about the spirit of debt is true. I believe you are concerned about my bills and that you want to help me eliminate them.

Lord, I ask you, in the name of Jesus, to break the spirit of debt from my life. I also ask you to cancel my debt miraculously.

Lord, I believe that as this man of God and I join our faith together, something special is being released into my life. I thank you that you have given me authority over the entire spirit world.

Right now, I boldly speak to the chief spirit, the spirit of debt that has been sent by the devil. In the mighty name of Jesus, I declare you to be bound. I break your hold on my life and on my finances! Spirit of debt, you can no longer operate in my life! In Jesus' name, you are firmly bound, and I am loosed from your power over me!

Father God, part the heavens for me. Let me know in my spirit that this foul spirit has been bound and defeated.

I now speak to the East, the West, the North, the South, that the ministering angels of God come forth and begin to release the abundance of God into my life. I boldly speak that miracles must begin to take place in my finances right now. In the name of Jesus, I accept my financial breakthrough.

Lord, I give you the glory for the financial miracles that are released into my life this day. Amen.

Say It Out Loud

Oh, child of God, say it out loud. "The power of the spirit of debt is broken from my life this day!" Say it again and again until it rings in the devil's ears. The spirit of debt has controlled your finances for the last day.

If you are married, go immediately and tell your spouse that the spirit of debt has been broken from your lives. Join together in proclaiming your financial victory.

If you are single, tell the next person you meet that the spirit of debt has been broken off your life.

If the Son therefore shall make you free, ye shall be free indeed.

John 8:36

6

Several Debt-Reduction Strategies

1. How to Sell a Home Rapidly

Sometimes your rapid debt-reduction strategy may call for the sale of your present house so that you can move to a home you can afford. In the following pages, you will find some helpful ideas for selling at a reasonable price in the shortest possible time.

Choose the Right Representative

It is usually easier for a realtor to sell your home than for you to sell it on your own. There are certain sales tools available to him which are not available to you. He has access to multiple listing services as well as other advertising methods. The dollars you spend on a *good* realtor's commission will be well worth it if he effects a fast sale at a fair price.

Your Agency Should Know Your Area

Your first priority in choosing the right company to represent you is to find an agency which has successfully sold other homes in your neighborhood. A little investigation will tell you which agents have made the most sales in your area in recent months. Remember, what you want is a *go-getter* who will work *for you.*

The more your agent knows about your particular area, the better. He should be able to tell prospective buyers about schools, churches, stores, parks, and a number of other things in your community. The realtor *must be sold on your neighborhood* before he can sell it to someone else. He should feel that your house is a good buy for anyone who fits into your price range.

Overpriced Means Overlooked

Remember, today's buyers are looking for a good deal. Your home won't sell *if you are asking too much for it.* Let your agent help you figure out a realistic selling price. This can be done by comparing recent sales in your area. There are dependable, mathematical formulas which will tell you how much your house should sell for. If you have a reputable realtor, you can trust the sale price he suggests.

A Few Dollars Spent Will Bring Big Money

You should be prepared to spend a little money to make your house stand out. It will cost you only three or four hundred dollars to make a real difference in your home's eye appeal. How your house looks from the curb can make a real difference to the buyer.

Touch up the outside paint, especially the trim. Wash the windows, and patch up cracks in the driveway and walkways. Be sure your yard is cleaned up and freshly mowed. Rake up the leaves, and clean leaves and other debris out of the gutter. If you have hedges, be sure they are neatly trimmed. Planting a few flowers along the walkway or around trees, or putting potted flowers on the porch will enhance the outside appearance tremendously.

Cleanliness Says, "Buy Me"

Do a major cleaning on the inside of the house. Your house makes a distinctive impression when the kitchen and bathrooms are spotless. Everything should be put away in its proper place, and if you have unnecessary furnishings, get rid of them. An uncluttered house looks cleaner and *more spacious.* Fill in any cracks in the walls with spackle, and repaint. Also, be sure to remove any spots from your carpet.

Put On a Good Show

Keep the following hints in mind when you have an appointment to show your home. *If the weather is hot,* turn on the air-conditioning far enough ahead of time to cool the entire house before the prospective buyer arrives. In cool weather, the temperature inside should be comfortable, but never too hot. Put soothing music on the stereo. A fresh flower arrangement always makes a room seem special, and you can create an inviting aroma by heating cinnamon in a potpourri pot.

Put your pets outdoors, and if you have a fenced yard, it is better to send small children outside, too. You don't want the buyer to be distracted or annoyed.

Make the house look bright by opening draperies and blinds and by turning on the lights in every room. These few, simple things can make your house feel like home to a prospective buyer.

Be Ready to Deal

Do not let the sale be stopped by an offer to purchase your house at a lower price equal to only a few mortgage payments. Keep in mind that your next payments may be almost all interest. If you let a buyer get away and have to wait three months for another one, *you make the next three mortgage payments.* Only a few dollars of those payments will go toward the pay-down of the principal.

When you decide to sell, it should be done as quickly as possible. Selling your home involves some technical aspects, so be sure you have proper professional representation.

2. How to Sell a Car Rapidly

In the process of selling the things you do not need, an automobile may be involved. Because of this possibility, I am writing this section to help you get the most money you can from the sale of your car. Every extra dollar you receive will help pay off your debt.

Prepare Your Car for Sale

Before you put your car on the market, *you must prepare it for sale.* Without a doubt, a car that looks good will sell more quickly and bring a higher price. As long as there is no rust or body work needed, *it should not cost more than a hundred dollars* to get your automobile looking great.

The first step is to *clean it thoroughly from top to tire, inside and out.* A dirty car has very little eye appeal, so a prospective buyer may be turned off before he even hears about how well it runs. This fact in itself makes it well worth the time and expense involved in *washing and waxing.*

A Clean Motor

Especially important is a clean engine. If you cannot afford to have your engine professionally steam cleaned, you can do it yourself at the jet-spray car wash. (Just be sure to protect electrical parts by completely covering them with plastic wrap.) *A clean engine usually looks almost brand new* and is a good selling point.

A Clean Interior

You can rent a steam cleaner to clean fabric upholstery and carpet on the car's interior. There are also special cleaning solutions for leather or vinyl. Small tears can be repaired with tape or vinyl repair solution of a matching color. If your vinyl top is showing its age, purchase some vinyl renewal spray to make it look like new. Also, remember to clean out the trunk and glove compartment. Be sure you have thoroughly cleaned all dust and dirt from the dashboard.

Set a Fair Price

At this point, you will be ready to set your price. Remember that *your car will sell more quickly if your asking price is fair.* To help you decide what is realistic, compare the following for a car of the same year and model as yours:

1. The price used-car dealers are asking.

2. The price private owners are asking in classified ads.

3. The blue-book value.

You should establish your price in the same range.

You Need Exposure

Once you have set the price, *exposure is the key ingredient. Advertise in the classified sections* of local newspapers and other publications. Ads should be short, catchy, and should clearly list your asking price. Also *place notices on bulletin boards* at the office, supermarket, church, or any other place you can. Keep a *For Sale* sign in the window, and *make sure your car is seen.* Drive it around and park it in conspicuous places. Make sure all your friends and relatives know your car is for sale. They can help you by keeping their ears and eyes open for potential buyers. You may even want to offer a small *finder's fee* to the person who refers the buyer to you.

Get Your Money

Once you have made the sale, it is best to *receive cash* for your car. If the buyer offers you a check, *go with him to his bank to cash it.* Be prepared to hand him the title as soon as you receive the cash or his check is cashed by his bank.

3. Don't Buy a Haunting House

The purchase of a home is the largest single investment the average person will ever make. It can be a blessing, or it can be a nightmare. *Don't let this very special purchase become a bad experience.* You must be careful not to buy a home that will *come back to haunt you.*

If your home turns out to be a *money pit,* you will never get out of debt. If it is located in an area which causes it to lose value, your rapid debt reduction will not be nearly so rewarding.

Get These Things Right

Location: There is an old real estate salesman's saying that every home buyer should know. There are three things that must be right before a piece of property is worth purchasing.

1. The *location* must be right.

2. It is important always to buy property in the right *location.*

3. Whatever you do, when you buy, be sure you buy in a good *location.*

Every house can be categorized by its price. There are inexpensive homes, as well as unbelievably expensive ones. In each price range, you can find homes in poor, fair, good, or excellent locations. Even if your present budget allows you to buy only the cheapest of homes, *buy it in the best location possible.*

Try to buy in a subdivision where most houses are more expensive than yours. When your house is the least expensive in the subdivision, *the higher priced homes will tend to pull up its value.* Just the opposite will take place if you buy the most expensive house in a subdivision. Your house will tend to pull up the value of the cheaper homes, *while theirs will tend to pull down the value of your home.*

If you have children or are planning a family, be sure your house is located in a *good school district.* Buy a home close to parks and shopping, but not too close. There should be several streets of housing between you and the hustle and bustle associated with such conveniences.

Choose your home in a location where the *property tax rate is not excessive.* Do not judge if taxes are high by the rate in your previous city. Always compare taxes according to the rates in the area where your new home purchase is being made.

If at all possible, choose a subdivision with a *sanitary sewer system.* Also seek out information about what is planned for the future in your area. If such things as a *prison* or a *sewage treatment plant* are scheduled, pass on that area. It will not be a good purchase.

Termites: Any house worth buying is worth spending the money for a *termite inspection.* There is a three-fold reason for this.

1. It will tell you if the house has termites. If it does and you choose to buy it anyway, as a condition of the purchase, stipulate that the seller exterminates all termites and repairs any damage they have done at *his cost, not yours.*

2. Most buyers *do have* termite inspections performed. At a later date, if you sell the house and did not have the previous termite problem taken care of by the former owner, you will have to pay for the extermination and repair for the person purchasing from you.

3. If there are termites in the home you buy, and they are not detected and eliminated, *they will eventually cost you big money.*

Electrical: The wiring in older homes is usually not adequate for today's modern appliances. There should be a complete inspection and test of all electrical switches, wiring, main power panel, and load capacity made by a licensed electrician. *Ask for a written report* with prices for repairs.

Plumbing: A certified plumber should inspect everything having to do with the plumbing and sewer. *Ask for a written report* with prices for repair.

Heating and Air-conditioning: Both the heating and cooling systems should be checked by a certified heating and air-conditioning specialist. Be sure to have the air flow to all rooms checked. *Ask for a written report* with prices for repair. Also keep in mind that heating and cooling costs can be extreme if you have excessively high ceilings.

Appliances: Ask for a guarantee on all appliances including dishwasher, garbage disposal, hot water heater, central vacuum, refrigerator, stove, and any built-ins. If any appliance is missing, for instance a stove or refrigerator, ask the seller to furnish you one at his cost. Don't be timid. The worst he can do is refuse.

You should have written warranty policies on all appliances. If written policies cannot be supplied, ask the seller to leave half the replacement cost for the appliances in an escrow account for six months. If all appliances are still operational at the end of that time, the money can then be released to the seller. If any must be repaired or replaced, the cost of replacement should come out of the escrow account.

Structural Compliance: You should ask the local building inspection department to have a building inspector meet you at the prospective house to answer questions and give you information. These are some of the questions he should answer for you.

Is the home *built according to code?* Is it *properly insulated?* Are there any *zoning violations* on the house? Are there any *zoning violations in the immediate neighborhood?* Have him explain any *zoning restrictions* that pertain to the area, such as no pets, no trucks allowed on the street, and other parking restrictions. You need to know everything you can about the house and neighborhood *before you buy. Have a written report made.*

Radon Gas Test: It has recently been discovered that there is a natural, radioactive gas called *radon* which seeps up through the ground and gets trapped inside houses. It is considered a *very dangerous gas.* There are properly certified companies which will test your prospective house for the presence of radon gas. *Ask for a written report* by a certified technician, with a price for eliminating the danger.

Garage: The most important thing about the garage is that both your automobiles fit into it comfortably. You need enough room to allow the car doors to be opened. You must also be able to get in and out of the garage with packages in hand. *Actually park both cars in the garage to see if they fit properly.*

Have the garage door and the automatic opener checked by a garage-door installation company. *Ask for a written report,* with a price to correct any problems.

Exterior Finishes: Brick is preferable on all exterior walls unless it is cost-prohibitive in your area; then the most practical and commonly used exterior finish should be considered. Vinyl or aluminum is preferred on trim. Exterior finishes of these materials will save you money year after year because they do not have to be painted. If the soffits and overhangs on your prospective house are not covered with aluminum or vinyl material, ask the seller if he will have them covered for you. If he will not, ask him if he will at least pay for half the cost. If he commits to paying any portion of the job, *get it in writing.* Then deduct that cost from the selling price of the house, and *have the job done only after you have received several bids.*

Drainage: Always find out all you can about storm drainage in the prospective subdivision. Ask the seller specifically if the house you are interested in has ever had drainage problems. Also ask several of the neighbors if the area drains well. Run water on the porches, driveway, and sidewalks to be sure it immediately flows *away from the house.* It can become a nightmare if water does not correctly drain off your property. If water flows toward the house, it will be expensive if not impossible to protect it at flood time.

Soil: Get a report from the local building inspection department as to whether or not the soil in your area is stable. If it contains bentonite or any other expanding soil, you must be assured that proper construction techniques were used to prevent the expansion of the soil from breaking the foundations. With this type of soil, there is also a real danger that the slab will rise or fall with the wet season. *It is better not to buy* if you cannot be assured that the soil is stable.

Earthquake Faults: These invisible fractures in the surface of the earth can be a real problem. They exist throughout the nation, *even in places where the earth doesn't shake.* Many faults creep and slip, causing tremendous damage to the homes above. Your building inspector should have knowledge of where these silent house-wrecking strata are.

Access: Check the traffic flow to and from the prospective house during rush hours. Notice if there is excessive traffic through the subdivision. Also check whether flooding ever closes roads to and from the area you are considering.

Fireplace: Always build a fire in the fireplace to see if the smoke is being properly drawn out of the house. Be sure the fireplace has a damper which operates correctly. Heating and cooling costs can be expensive if the fireplace damper does not function properly.

You should also have a reputable chimney sweep inspect for creosote buildup and loose fire tiles or brick. *Get a written report* with estimates for repairs or cleaning.

Cabinets and Closets: Be sure the cupboard space in the kitchen is ample to meet your family's requirements. You must be able to store *all* your dishes, utensils, and other kitchen items. Just because the cupboards seem to meet the needs of the seller, that does not mean they will be adequate for your needs. Take stock of each cabinet and be sure the space is sufficient. Also check the closet space. You should be able to hang your clothes without your garments hitting the back of the closet wall. You also want to be sure the house has enough extra closet or attic space for storage of your seasonal items.

Easements: Have all easements on the property *clearly identified.* Have some small pegs driven about ten feet apart on all easement lines so that you can see exactly how much of your yard is dedicated to utilities. An easement could stop you from building onto your house, or could keep you from adding a pool or patio at a later date. It could also cause the inconvenience of equipment being moved across your property from time to time.

Eminent Domain: Through eminent domain, the government has the right to buy your property, *whether or not you wish to sell it.* Be sure there are no future plans for a freeway or other projects across your land. Government agencies often tend to offer less than fair market price when they take over property. Also realize that if a freeway is scheduled to come through the subdivision, or a road is to be widened, property values will usually be drastically reduced, even if your house remains, because of the noise and the undesirability of living next to heavy traffic.

Curbs and Sidewalks: If the curbs and sidewalks adjacent to the home are in poor condition, at some future time your city may decide to repair them. When they do, *you may be billed for the cost.* This is also true if your subdivision has no sidewalks. You may be required to pay the bill when they are added at a later date.

Municipal Services: Check to see that proper services are available. You need to know if there is *garbage collection* at the curb, or if you are required to haul your own trash off to the dump. This hauling can become expensive and inconvenient over a long period of time. Also investigate the condition of the local roads in your area. Are they well maintained or full of potholes? If you are a commuter, you need to know about the reliability and easy access to buses or train service in the area.

Roof: Have a reputable roofing contractor or engineer check the condition of the roof. Do not rely on the realtor to do this for you. The roof is one of the most expensive things to replace. If it leaks, severe damage may be done to the structure and contents of the home. Ask the inspector to state the probable number of years the roof will last. Then carefully consider if you will be ready to replace it at that time. If not, have the seller replace it or share this upcoming expense with you. Be sure to *get a written report* of repair and replacement cost.

Swimming Pool: If the house has a swimming pool, have a certified pool repair company examine the pool and its plumbing, wiring, and motors. *Ask for a written report* of its condition and the cost of necessary repairs.

Crime Report: Check with the local police department about the crime rate in the area. Find out if there is any problem with juvenile delinquency. *These problems almost always grow worse with time.*

In general, take the time to check every possible thing pertaining to your prospective house. By doing this, you will help guarantee that you do not buy a *haunting house.*

4. Buying Insurance

No matter what type of insurance you need, there are several things you must consider before you buy. If you will carefully look at the following points, you will be more likely to purchase the coverage which best meets your needs. Remember, *whatever you save in insurance premiums should be used to pay down your debt.*

Consult a financial advisor. He will best know your individual situation and provide you with additional advice on applying the following suggestions.

1. To the best of your ability, determine exactly *how much insurance you need.* You are throwing your money down the drain when you pay for unnecessary, extra coverage.

2. Always *shop around for the best buy.* Compare different policies and prices. Investigate what both company salespeople and independent agents have to offer.

3. Never let your agent decide what you should buy. He will be able to give you advice, but remember, *he can offer you only the coverage he sells.* That may not be what you need or want. Also, because he is paid primarily on a commission basis, he may tend to sell you more than you really need. Do not hesitate to tell one agent the price quote you received from another to see if he can give you a better deal.

4. Always *buy the highest deductible you can afford to pay.* The purpose of insurance is to protect you from serious financial loss, not to pay for things you can easily afford yourself. The higher your deductible rate, the lower your premium will be. It is smarter to agree to pay a few small expenses out of your own pocket than to pay unreasonably high premiums.

5. Never buy *a policy you don't understand.* Your policy should be written in *plain language* so that you can see exactly what is covered and what is not covered.

6. Whenever possible, *make your premium payments once a year.* In most cases this will cost you less than paying semi-annually, quarterly, or monthly.

7. *Don't be afraid to investigate* a prospective insurance company. Find out if they are licensed to do business in your state. From their financial statement, determine if they are financially sound. Check with friends and other customers to see if the company *promptly pays claims.* Also check if they tend to adjust rates upward after a claim is filed. The agent should be able to give you the names of some customers you can call *for a personal recommendation.*

8. Every time you renew your policy, or at least once a year, *re-evaluate your coverage* to be sure it still meets all your needs.

Homeowner's Insurance

Most homeowner's policies insure your house, property, and personal belongings. They also give you liability coverage in the event someone suffers bodily injury or property damage on your premises. If you own your home, *you should have homeowner's insurance.*

It is generally recommended by the insurance industry that you cover your house for 80 percent of its *replacement value.* Keep in mind, this is not the same as its market value. Replacement value is the dollar amount it would cost you to *rebuild* your home at today's prices. If you allow your insurance coverage to drop below 80 percent of replacement value, the company is not obligated to pay the entire cost of replacement. *They may actually make you responsible for a percentage of the loss.*

To decide the proper amount of coverage for your *personal property,* you should *make a complete inventory of your belongings* to determine their dollar value. Please realize that unless otherwise stated, they are insured only for their *cash value, not their replacement value.* In other words, a piece of furniture that cost you $1,000 five years ago may have a cash value of only $20 today due to depreciation. If you want *replacement* coverage for your personal belongings, you must pay more money for it. You must also be sure your policy clearly states that *your belongings will be replaced.*

If you have valuables such as jewelry, furs, or original art, they may not be fully covered under your homeowner's policy. Talk to your agent and determine if it is worth the extra cost to insure these items separately for their full replacement value.

Once you have determined what dollar amount of insurance you need, *begin to shop for discounts.* Some companies offer discounts for certain safety features such as fire extinguishers, smoke detectors, dead-bolt locks, and burglar alarms. Also, many companies offer a discount if your home is new or nearly new.

Tenant's Insurance

If you rent your home, it is wise to buy *tenant's insurance* to cover your personal property. If you live in a condominium or cooperative, your association fees may already be paying for insurance on a portion of your property. Find out how much coverage the association provides. Then buy only as much additional insurance as you need to make up the difference. Do not leave it to chance. Always be sure your home and personal property are fully covered.

Automobile Insurance

Automobile insurance rates vary greatly from area to area. One of the first things you can do to cut this cost is to *eliminate duplicate coverage.* If you already have a good health insurance policy, find out if your state requires you to purchase additional medical coverage on your automobile insurance. If not, your attorney or financial consultant may advise you to drop the medical portion from your policy. (Keep in mind that if you carry passengers other than those covered by your medical policy, you do need to be sure they are properly covered.)

If you have life insurance, there is no need for death benefits on your automobile policy. Also, if you have some form of disability insurance, you probably will not need additional disability or wage loss coverage unless your state requires it.

If you belong to a motor club, towing costs are usually covered, so there is no need to add this coverage to your automobile policy. In fact, even if these costs are not covered in some other way, consider paying them yourself if they are needed. They are generally less expensive when paid on an *as-needed basis* than paying the additional insurance premium.

When you decide how much collision coverage you need, keep in mind the insurer will reimburse you only for the *cash value* of your car. This rule holds true even if you have insured your car for a high dollar amount. Remember, it is the value of your automobile after depreciation that will be covered, so don't buy any more coverage than the replacement cost.

Another savings can be realized if you keep in mind that your collision insurance may cover you when you drive a rented car. Check your policy to be sure. If you are covered, you can waive this additional charge from the rental agency.

Shop for Discounts

Once you have determined the amount of automobile insurance you need, remember to shop for discounts. They are offered for a variety of reasons too numerous to list here.

Lock in the Rate

Always have your policy written with a twelve-month rate, even if you're paying your premium every six months. The rates on a six-month policy can be raised twice a year. Unless otherwise stated, the rates on a twelve-month plan cannot be increased during the term of the policy.

Some companies return a dividend to their customers at the end of each year when state-wide claims have remained low. This return amounts to a reduction in your premium cost. Be sure you allow some of these companies to bid for your coverage.

Also, be sure to inform your agent immediately if there is any change of status which will lower your rate. For instance, if you move from the city to the country, or if you drop a young driver from your policy, your rates possibly will be reduced.

Always check the insurance rates of a new automobile before buying it. A good sale price for a fancy sports car is not a good deal if you cannot afford to have it insured.

Life Insurance

Life insurance is designed to protect your dependents from the problems they would suffer should they lose your income. Its purpose should be to provide a way for them to maintain their current lifestyle in your absence. The amount of protection you buy should be based primarily on what your family's needs will be in the foreseeable future.

If there are two wage earners in the family, then both should be insured. A younger couple will usually need more life insurance than senior citizens who no longer have children to support.

To decide just how much life insurance coverage you need, your first step is to calculate your family's current expenses. Now, subtract any expenses which would be eliminated by your death. Also, if your beneficiaries qualify for any social security benefits at your death, deduct this amount. Then deduct any life insurance you may already have through your employer or elsewhere.

You now have a good indicator of how much coverage you need to buy.

The least expensive life insurance is usually group coverage. Also keep in mind that it is more economical to buy one large policy than several smaller ones. For instance, a $100,000 policy is normally less expensive than two $50,000 policies.

The two primary types of life insurance are *term* and *whole life.*

Term Insurance

Term insurance is not a savings or investment plan. It is life insurance and nothing more. Compared to whole life, it is not very expensive in the early years. However, as you grow older, the premiums usually increase. At the same time, the value of the policy may decrease. Most of these policies are good only until you reach a specified age.

Since your insurance needs may decrease as you grow older, term insurance could still be the best buy for you. Most term insurance policies allow you to exchange them for whole life insurance at a later date. This is called "guaranteed insurability."

Whole Life Insurance

As long as you faithfully pay the premium, a whole life insurance policy covers you for your entire life. This type of policy has the ability to build up a cash value as you grow older. The longer you maintain the policy, the more cash value it gains up to its maturity date. For this reason, many people maintain whole life policies as savings accounts. However, past experience indicates this is not the best way to save money.

Whole life is expensive in the early years, but the premiums do not increase. With certain types of policies, you are required to pay the premium for only a specified number of years, or until you reach a certain age. At that point, the policy is paid in full, and your coverage continues.

Your Policy Can Reduce Your Debt

If you already have a whole life policy, you might be able to use it to reduce your debt. A policy with a high cash value can be cashed out. A portion of the proceeds can be used to buy a less expensive policy, and the balance can be used to pay off some or all of your bills.

Also, many older whole life policies will allow you to borrow against them at *a very low rate of interest,* perhaps as low as 5 or 6 percent, depending on when they were purchased. If that interest rate is lower than the interest you are paying on your current debts, you may want to use this method to pay your bills. Remember! *Whatever you do, don't leave your family unprotected.* If you cash in a policy, *the protection stops. It is up to you* to be sure you have adequate life insurance coverage at all times.

Health Insurance

In today's high-cost society, it is important to have a good health insurance policy. However, there are so many variables to consider in this type of coverage that it cannot be explained in this book. I advise you to shop around and discuss the many types of health insurance with several reputable agents to find the policy which best suits your needs.

5. How to Advertise in the Classified Section

If you have surplus items that can be sold to generate more cash, you may wish to advertise them in the classified section of your local newspaper. By following a few simple instructions, writing a classified ad can be easy. Your objective is simply to tell the customer:

1. *What you are selling.* Be specific. Don't make the buyer guess.

2. *Something special about the item.* Tell the buyer why your item is better than the other twenty just like it.

3. *About its condition.* Let the buyer know if it is almost brand new, excellent, fair, or good.

4. *The price you are asking.* Most people are shopping for a specific item in a particular price range. They appreciate knowing if your item is within their range without calling to ask. *Don't waste their time or yours.* List your price.

5. *A phone number.* Let people call you to ask questions. Then if they sound really interested, give them your address. *Unless you are having a garage sale,* it is not necessary to put your address in the ad.

Get some good ideas about what to say by reading a few classified ads in your local newspaper and noting the ones that *grab* your attention.

Your ad may say something like this:

86 Astro Van. Custom interior. New tires. Only 25,000 miles. Excellent condition. $8000. 777-7777 days, 333-3333 after 6.

When you place your ad, the representative from the publication will help you with details such as abbreviating common words and how to say the most for the least amount of money. *Don't be afraid to ask for help.*

6. How to Have a Money-Making Garage Sale

A garage sale can be a worthwhile means of helping to pay down your total debt. Don't be afraid. It's not too hard, once you know how.

The Best Days

Generally, weekends are the best times for garage sales — Friday, Saturday, or Sunday. Two-day sales give *twice* the opportunity to make money.

Fridays seem to be the best days because the children are in school, Dad is working, and many moms are free to go treasure hunting. Some people set aside Fridays just for rummaging. Also remember that Friday is payday for most people.

Although many people have other things to do, Saturdays can still be excellent sale days. For those who work during the week, Saturdays and Sunday afternoons are the only days available.

A few people always have sales in the middle of the week because they feel they have less competition, and everyone who is bargain hunting will be sure to come.

Long holiday weekends are usually not the best times for a sale. Many families make specific plans or go out of town. Even those who are driving around during these days are usually going somewhere special. Generally, this time is not conducive to a successful sale. However, if you are fortunate enough to live on the main road to the lake or local tourist attraction, you will have a *captive audience* on holidays. Many travelers won't be able to resist stopping to see your wares.

The Best Season

Unless you are fortunate enough to live where it is perpetually spring, the best times of the year seem to be late spring, late summer, or early fall. More people are out and about during these times. Extreme temperatures or rain do not provide the best setting for a successful sale, so avoid these conditions if at all possible.

Also remember that just before school starts, many mothers are looking for quality, used school clothing.

The Best Time

Most customers can't get to your sale before 8:00 a.m. However, many collectors and antique shop buyers fiercely compete to find the real treasures. They will usually show up as early as you want to open your sale. Many are up when their newspapers arrive. They read the ads and carefully select the route they can take to hit the most sales in the shortest time. If you open before full daylight, you *must* have excellent lighting on your merchandise, or your customers will soon be on their way.

Generally, most of your customers will have come and gone by mid-afternoon. If you have nothing else you must do, it can sometimes pay to leave your sale open until around 5:00 p.m. Don't close up too early, for you may get a late customer who will purchase a lot of your *leftovers*.

In some communities it is becoming common for working people to hold evening sales in the summer. These sales begin around 6:30 p.m. and continue until 9:00, or dark. This schedule can bring in a completely different crowd. Those who work during the day, those who are out for a drive, and evening walkers often like to stop and browse.

Advertising

Proper advertising can make the difference in whether or not your sale is successful. Be sure people know what you are offering and how to find you. An advertisement in the garage-sales column of your local newspaper should be brief, but enticing. Be sure to list a few of your most interesting items, your opening time, and complete address. Give easy directions if you are out of the way.

Such items as baby clothes and furnishings, antiques and collectibles, tools, or furniture are often sought after and should be mentioned in your ad. Also place your ad in your neighborhood weekly tabloid. These ads are usually inexpensive but require advance notice, so plan ahead.

A large sign with "Garage Sale" and your address should be placed at all main intersections leading to your house and also in your front yard. (Check local regulations regarding placement of signs.) Using black paint or waterproof markers, neatly print your sign in letters large enough to be easily read a half block away. If possible, have someone check periodically to be sure your signs are still in place, especially if the day is quite breezy.

If entrance to your sale cannot be seen from the street, another sign should be placed in your yard indicating "Back Yard" or other directions. It is advisable to have some part of your sale *clearly visible* if possible. People hesitate to stop if they do not see an open garage door or a yard full of sale items.

You can also attract attention with helium-filled balloons tied to your signs and strips of colorful banners in your front yard. This gives your sale an inviting, carnival-like atmosphere. If you are really ambitious, you can make scarecrow-type signs from two pieces of wood draped with a dress, topped with a hat, and your sale sign stapled to the arm.

Put your signs up the night before, or in the early morning of your sale day. If you have time and your sale is large, you may wish to put up handbills on bulletin boards at your neighborhood supermarkets, laundromats, or churches. (Be courteous and *remove all signs* as soon as your sale ends.) Handbills delivered to the people in your neighborhood will also help stir interest.

Scout the Competition

If you are not a regular garage sale customer, it will pay to spend two or three weekends scouting such events for ideas. At least try to get up early on a Friday or Saturday morning and stop at several sales. You will learn a lot about pricing, display of goods, and advertising. Tell everyone you know that you are getting ready to have your own sale, and ask for their experienced advice. Most people love to help by giving you ideas.

Trash or Treasure — Be Sure You Know

You have heard that "one man's trash is another man's treasure." Be sure what you consider *trash* isn't actually a *treasure* before you sell it too cheaply. A visit to your local flea market should educate you. Those old, chipped enamel kitchen utensils you remember your mom using, and the ugly little Christmas ornaments Grandma had *may be worth a small fortune.* Old baseball cards, comics, Valentine cards, banks, kitchenware, glassware, quilts, vintage clothing and jewelry are often highly sought after. (In fact, if you have a lot of this type of merchandise, including some antique furniture, you might do well to hold a well-advertised *auction.* Collectors and dealers bidding against each other can sometimes raise prices unbelievably high.)

Ready to Get Ready

Now you are ready to get ready for your sale. How do you display your merchandise? *Neatness counts in a big way.* Toys should be clean and all pieces included. Clothing should be clean, ironed, and plainly priced and sized. Glassware and kitchenware need to be free of grease and dust. Remember, if you wouldn't want to buy it and clean it up, others will probably feel the same way.

Be sure you have plenty of table space and have all items neatly displayed and legibly priced. Household bric-a-brac, records, books, and such should be priced under a dollar. Exceptions include Elvis and other collectible *oldies* record albums, and very old collectible books and cookbooks. These may bring considerably more money. Appliances and electronics will bring up to one-third retail value if in good condition. If clothing is currently in style and in excellent condition, you may get up to one-fourth retail value.

Helpful Hints

You should have about thirty dollars in cash in your *bank* at the start of your sale. Most of it should be in one-dollar bills. You should also have about five dollars in change, mostly quarters.

Keep jewelry and smaller valuable collectibles near you in order to be able to watch them carefully. Yes, unfortunately, some people do steal, even at garage sales.

You may want to bring out a pot of coffee or lemonade and cookies. A snack will help you ward off hunger during the sale.

Have plenty of paper and pens handy. If people wish to leave lower bids on certain items, you will be able to let them jot down their phone numbers. If you have a small adding machine with tape, plug it in near your cash box. It will be really handy to accurately total a long list of items. If you are selling any electrical items, have an electrical outlet or extension cord nearby so that customers can test them. If you provide a private corner for trying on clothing, be sure to monitor how many garments go in and out. Some people have been known to hide clothing under their outer clothes while in the dressing room.

If your merchandise doesn't seem to be moving as fast as you would like, you can always tack up a "No Reasonable Offer Refused" sign, or "Half-Price Sale Today" banner on the second day. You may also want to haggle. If someone offers you $5 for an item marked $10, you can counter with a price of $7.50. You may want to put several miscellaneous items in a *free* box just to get rid of them. It also works wonders if you have a box of toys or trinkets to give small children something to do, so that their mothers can shop in peace.

Watch Your Cash

Be sure to keep a *close watch* on your cash box at all times, and carry it with you if you must go inside and no one is helping you. If you have a large sale, you really do need a *helper*, especially during the *early rush* of customers. Determine ahead of time if you are willing to accept checks. If so, be sure they are drawn on local banks and the writer has a picture I.D. The phone number should be included on the check, *especially on big-ticket items.*

Figure Your Profit

After the sale is over, don't forget to deduct your starting cash and your advertising costs from your total intake to determine your net profit. *You will probably be pleasantly surprised* at how well you did!

John Avanzini was born in Paramaribo, Surinam, South America, in 1936. He grew up and was educated in Texas, and received his doctorate in philosophy from Baptist Christian University, Shreveport, Louisiana. Dr. Avanzini now resides with his wife, Patricia, in Fort Worth, Texas, where he is the Director of His Image Ministries.

Dr. Avanzini's television program, "Principles of Biblical Economics," airs five times per day, seven days per week, on more than 550 television stations from coast to coast. He speaks nationally and internationally in conferences and seminars every week. His ministry is worldwide, and many of his vibrant teachings are now available in tape and book form.

Dr. Avanzini is an extraordinary teacher of the Word of God, bringing forth many of the present truths that God is using in these days to prepare the Body of Christ for His triumphant return.

To share your testimony with John Avanzini,
you may write:

**John Avanzini
Attn: Partner Love Center
P.O. Box 917001
Fort Worth, Texas 76117-9001**

Other Books by John Avanzini

Always Abounding
Enter a new dimension of abundant living through a
plan from God's Word that cannot fail. **$5.95**

Faith Extenders
Study how characters from the Bible caused their faith
to grow, and how the same methods can increase your
faith today. **$7.95**

Hundredfold
See clearly and thoroughly the scriptural laws of
seed-time and harvest, God's plan for your
increase. **$7.95**

It's Not Working, Brother John!
If you've done all you know and still haven't received
God's promises, study these 25 things that close the
windows of heaven. **$8.95**

John Avanzini Answers Your Questions
Find the answers to the 20 most-often-asked questions
about biblical economics. **$6.95**

Moving the Hand of God
Discover how you can get God's attention focused on
your most urgent need. **$6.95**

Powerful Principles of Increase
Find out how you can take the resources of this world to
establish God's Kingdom. **$8.95**

Stolen Property Returned
Learn how to take the thief to the heavenly courtroom, and recover what he has stolen. **$5.95**

The Wealth of the World
Find help to prepare for your part in the great end-time harvest of souls and wealth. **$6.95**

The Financial Freedom Series

War on Debt
Financial Freedom Series, Volume I — If you are caught in a web of debt, your situation is not hopeless. You can break the power of the spirit of debt. **$7.95**

Rapid Debt-Reduction Strategies
Financial Freedom Series, Volume II — Learn practical ways to pay off all your debts — mortgage included — in record time. **$12.95**

The Victory Book
Financial Freedom Series, Volume III — This workbook takes you step by step through "The Master Plan" for paying off every debt. **$14.95**

Have a Good Report
Financial Freedom Series, Volume IV — Find out what your credit report says about you, and learn the steps that will help you correct the negative information. **$8.95**

**Complete both sides of this
order form to receive a 10% discount
on your book order.**

Qty	Title	Cost	Total
	Always Abounding	5.95	
	Faith Extenders	7.95	
	Financial Excellence	9.95	
	Hundredfold	7.95	
	It's Not Working, Brother John!	8.95	
	John Avanzini Answers Questions	6.95	
	Moving the Hand of God	6.95	
	Powerful Principles of Increase	8.95	
	Stolen Property Returned	5.95	
	The Wealth of the World	6.95	
	War on Debt	7.95	
	Rapid Debt-Reduction Strategies	12.95	
	The Victory Book	14.95	
	Have a Good Report	8.95	
	Subtotal		
	Less 10% Discount		
	Shipping & Handling		2.00
	Total Enclosed		

(   ) Enclosed is my check or money order made
        payable to **HIS Publishing Company**

Please charge my: (   ) Visa   (   ) MasterCard

(   ) Discover   (   ) American Express

Account # ☐☐☐☐☐☐☐☐☐☐☐☐☐☐☐☐

Expiration Date   _____ / _____ / _____

Signature_____

To assure prompt and accurate delivery of your order,
please take the time to print all information neatly.

Name_____

Address_____

City_____State_____Zip_____

Area Code & Phone (_____)_____

Send mail orders to:

HIS Publishing Company

P.O. Box 917001

Fort Worth, TX 76117-9001